Your Faith

Memorial?
Memory? or Miracle?

David Bena

Dorothy

May God strengthen
you continually!

+ Dane

Your Faith

Memorial?
Memory? or Miracle?

David Bena

FORWARD MOVEMENT PUBLICATIONS
CINCINNATI, OHIO

The Holy Bible: Revised Standard Version. Thomas Nelson & Sons, New York, 1952.

The Message—The New Testament in Contemporary English by Eugene Peterson. Navpress, Colorado Springs, CO, 1993.

The Book of Common Prayer. The Church Hymnal Corporation, New York, 1979.

The Taste of New Wine by Keith Miller. Word Books, Waco, TX, 1965.

Church Growth and the Power of Evangelism by Howard Hanchey. Cowley Publications, Cambridge, MA, 1990.

©2003 Forward Movement Publications
412 Sycamore Street, Cincinnati, Ohio 45202
1-800-543-1813
www.forwardmovement.org

Table of Contents

Introduction

It was drippingly hot. A young Marine captain sat on the ground under the shade of an Asian Pine, 9 o'clock in the morning and the temperature already at 105 degrees. He sat there in the shade, sweating and exhausted. He had spent the first half of the previous night on a bombing mission over North Vietnam. Then, after returning from his mission and just on the edge of falling asleep, he had been awakened by the "kathump" of a mortar round leaving its tube in the nearby mountains. Several others followed. The captain knew that in a few seconds his world would be exploding with mortars lobbed in by the enemy. Scurrying into the bunker beside his Quonset hut, he had spent several more hours shivering in the cold, hardened bunker. Here he was—9 a.m.—too tired to sleep. Might as well get some reading in.

So he was now sitting on the ground lost in a book. The title of the book was *The Taste of New Wine* by Keith Miller. A relatively new book on the market, it had been sent to Vietnam as one of many the chaplains packed in their gear to give out to personnel. The captain was devouring this one. It was giving him a road map. As he sat reading the book, he realized that it was moving him through previously uncharted territory—how to fill the vacant "God spot" in his heart. He read the whole book in one sitting. And when he got up off the ground and walked back to his hut, he was a different man.

That Marine was me. So many years ago, God used Keith Miller's book to show me the way to a relationship with God, and my life was changed forever. Now, over 30 years later, I am writing a book. Perhaps this one will help you just as *New Wine* helped me so many years ago. The vacant "God spot" in my life has been filled to overflowing, and it feels good! Might you be filled as well in a whole new and meaningful way?

The stories I put on these pages are based on situations with which I have been involved over the years. Names, locations, and circumstances have in many cases been altered to protect anyone from being identified. In no instance have I included any confessional or confidential material.

Many people assisted me in writing this book. Keith Miller helped me immeasurably—motivating me to keep writing, gently advising me on writing styles, editing and re-editing what came out of my head onto paper, and kept my focus on the faith treasure hunt aspects of this book. Two other friends, Pat Merriam and Gene Garber, poured over the manuscript and helped me organize the material. My bishop and friend, Dan Herzog, gave me some great feedback. Two of my most trusted friends, Tom Brownfield and Bill Johnson, both former Marines, gave me invaluable advice. And the Forward Movement Staff was right there all the way to publication and beyond! But mostly I thank my wife and life partner, Mary Ellen, for inspiring me to deeper faith, and for encouraging me to write about it.

—*David Bena*

Foreword

If you are interested in the revitalization of the parish church or your own life, I recommend *Your Faith: Memorial? Memory? or Miracle?* to you. The author, David Bena, is the genuine article. He won't settle for less than the truth. He is straight-forward and direct, which might be expected from a former Marine who flew more than 250 combat missions as bombardier/navigator on an A-6A low-level attack bomber. He also knows and loves the Church, having been a parish priest, an Air Force chaplain, and now the Bishop Suffragan of the Episcopal Diocese of Albany, New York. All these experiences have sensitized David, the person, into a thoughtful, kind man who cares especially for people searching for ways to grow, and to love and serve God more effectively.

Bishop Bena sees today's spiritual issues of "reality" and "relevance" from a fresh perspective. I've seen him wrestle with and move through many of the problems and opportunities described in these pages. And now this searcher for truth and the reality of God brings his honest approach to those who have wondered why their lives or their churches seem stagnant and gray.

Here is a simple, candid analysis for individual Christians and church leaders, a way to diagnose your own underlying assumptions, spiritual development, and those of the churches in which you worship and learn. I believe the re-examination work the Bishop suggests is essential for churches to become a living, loving family in any real sense. This is true because the nature and spiritual temperature of these mostly unexamined "underlying assumptions" determine the content and emotional tone of the entire enterprise of the church. The secular world's take on the relevance, integrity, and love of God through the Church is at stake in this kind of analysis.

Bena explains how education, worship, and evangelism taught and practiced in the local church will vary widely according to whether a church is focused on:

◆ Memorializing and preserving the God story as a real but past event;

◆ Remembering and re-describing one's earlier life-changing conversion experiences; or

◆ Growing and changing, consciously addressing every activity and block to loving they discover to a living, interactive, personal God, who is *present* in all educational groups, worship services, and relationships on a minute-by-minute basis.

Here Bena clarifies how the assumptions you—or your church—live by determines the direction and strength of every activity and attitude expressed in your life together. Here is a way to begin to take stock. You can start to make realistic decisions about what to do, and how to begin to change and grow in the ability to receive and spread God's kind of love.

I heartily recommend *Your Faith: Memorial? Memory? or Miracle?* to people who love the Church, but are discouraged about its lethargy; to those who have a love/hate relationship with the Church. This book is also seeking people, in and out of the Church, who would like to learn how to live for God from a courageous man, a man who wound up being a bishop for the God who found him and gave him hope.

— *J. Keith Miller*
Austin, Texas

Author of *The Taste of New Wine, A Hunger for Healing, What To Do With The Rest of Your Life,* and other books.

Faith

Chapter One

Faith—
A Gift From God

Direct us, O Lord, in all our doings with your most gracious favor, and further us with your continual help; that in all our works begun, continued, and ended in you, we may glorify your holy Name, and finally, by your mercy, obtain everlasting life; through Jesus Christ our Lord. Amen.

The Book of Common Prayer, 832

Your Faith—Handle With Prayer

Remember walking out the door of your home as a teenager, and hearing Mom or Dad yell, "Be careful!"? It is a standard parting line used by parents all over the world. "Be careful" is actually good advice to follow not only when we leave the house as teenagers, but also when, as adults, we examine our faith. If we are not careful in dealing with our belief system, we can end up confused and befuddled about our core values. But if we handle our faith with care, we can find fulfillment in life both now and in the hereafter.

This is a book about faith. And not just faith in general. It is about *your* faith—your faith in God. I wish to walk along beside you for awhile as you take a good look at your faith in God, your system of making sense of a world which often seems like a lot of nonsense. What is the system you cling to for ultimate meaning? If your faith is in God, what does that faith look like? And, will it go the distance for you? Does your faith have a biblical basis? Or, is it based on something less focused? Is your faith living and breathing, sailing swiftly before the wind? Or, is it slowly sinking into the seas of uncertainty or cynicism? These are serious questions, questions we are slow to address with others.

What I am doing here, as I walk along beside you in this book, is holding up some concepts and stories for you to examine and see if they fit your pilgrimage. I will share some of my own faith journey, hoping that sharing my journey will assist you in yours.

I believe that in the present culture of the Church there are three stages in Faith Development: Memorial Faith, Memory Faith, and Miracle Faith. As this book progresses we will unpack each stage and examine it closely. I have observed that people, including myself, sometimes get hung up in a particular stage of Faith, and become paralyzed—sometimes spiritually, sometimes emotionally. The paralysis can go on for years—or even a lifetime; trapping us and keeping us from growing! We are like the little boy who has climbed up into a tree and finds it much too scary to climb back down. But he does not want to lose face with his friends, so he won't call for help. He just sits up there in that tree all day long. He is trapped. Ever been there?

So I will focus on the three stages of Faith just mentioned—Memorial Faith, Memory Faith, and Miracle Faith. Here are some keys—let's unlock the packages! I believe that we people of faith get stuck in either the Memorial Faith stage or the Memory Faith stage, and never get to the Miracle Faith stage where we find the peace that St. Paul speaks of as "passing all understanding." Maybe we have experienced a miracle-like view of God, either through a rich liturgical experience or a strong evangelical sermon, and we sensed peace in our life for the first time. But somehow, it didn't seem to take! Soon after the experience, we found that we were right back where we had started. Or that after the experience we were in a different place than we were before, but now we were just as unsettled as before. It is not until we get to the Miracle Faith stage that we can integrate the positive aspects of Memorial Faith and Memory Faith, and allow the vacuum in our soul to be perfectly filled by God.

Let's walk along together and look at each stage. I'll begin by telling you my story. I'll stop at each stage of faith as I encountered it and explain how each impacted my life.

After I have shown you an example of each stage of faith from my life, we'll walk more specifically through each stage. Chapter-by-chapter, I will give you the high and low points of each stage. Finally we'll reach the goal of our walk together—Miracle Faith!

In a nutshell here are the Three Stages of Faith:

Memorial Faith. The faith of ritual; the faith of the mind; the faith we have inherited; the faith often seen in liturgical churches.

Memory Faith. The faith of an experience; the faith of the heart; the faith we have discovered; the faith often seen in evangelical churches.

Miracle Faith. The faith of adventure; the faith of total commitment to the living and loving God; the faith of growth; the faith of the Bible; the faith seen in all kinds of churches where people have broken through and seen the Miracle of God-in-action.

Ready for a walk?

Chapter Two

My Journey—
It All Started So Well

The Building of Memorial Faith

I have been down a lot of faith roads in my life. Many led to box canyons! Let me share with you what happened to me on my way to adulthood—Memorial Faith.

A Roman Catholic church on the side of a hill in a river town in upstate New York . . . a large farm house with a few barns on a country road close to the river town . . . a small public school filled with kids whose families faithfully took them to church every Sunday, and whose teachers would freely call parents if a student was getting into trouble . . . a family of two parents, a grandfather, and six kids.

I have just described my childhood environment. I grew up "protected." We had a home, food, clothes, money, and lots of love. As a small child, I learned my night prayers by heart—the Lord's Prayer, the Hail Mary, the Act of Contrition, the Apostles' Creed, the Angelus, and finally the closing prayer that stated, "*Take my body, Jesus—eyes and ears and tongue. Never let them, Jesus, help to do Thee wrong. Take my heart and fill it, full of love for Thee. All I have, I give Thee. Give Thyself to me.*" What a powerful prayer for a child! By the time I was five, I had all my prayers memorized, and said them faithfully every night before falling asleep. Harry Truman and then

Dwight Eisenhower were the presidents in those growing-up years. Everyone in our town knew these presidents believed in God—they said things like, "God bless America," during their speeches, and they went to church every Sunday. We believed they were honest and good politicians commissioned to protect the American way of life. There was a sense of stability on the home front. We knew we could contain Communism, and the Roman Catholic Church was very active in praying for its downfall. My two oldest brothers served in the Korean War, and my third brother served in the Lebanon Crisis. We prayed for them while they were away in the service. Our family went to Mass faithfully each Sunday. God was up there in His heaven and we were down here praying for our souls. On Sunday, we would gather in the beautiful old brick church on the side of the hill—Father Gaisley droning on in Latin, nuns often making up the choir, incense filling the cavernous nave with a sweet smelling aroma, and *sanctus* bells calling us to attention as the Host and Chalice were raised.

This was my childhood religious world. In many ways, it was idyllic. I felt "protected." Everything would come out right if you said your prayers, went to confession, and tried as hard as possible to be good. There was just one problem for me: although my faith was very ritualistic and ordered, it was not very personal. I did not perceive God as being near me. God was up there. I was down here.

So although I felt protected by the system, I did not feel particularly close to God. I just did the best I could with what I had, which proved to be not good enough. What I had was Memorial Faith, the faith of ritual. I went through the motions because generations before me had gone through those same motions. So I was faithfully taught the way of Mother Church. The great Memorial Faith of the Church seemed to tell me that if you did the rituals, followed the many rules, and said the prayers, you stood a pretty good chance of doing a little time in purgatory before slipping into heaven.

I began to think that although others before me may have lived their religion this way and felt close to God, it didn't seem to be working for me. I didn't know how to get close to God, and I didn't think I should talk about it with anyone because I judged that talking about it might make me look stupid or flawed. So while I continued to say my night prayers faithfully, I was not making a connection with a loving, personal God. Eventually I began to question the validity of the system as I had understood it.

Thus began a double life for me. On the one hand, I lived a ritualistic, religious, Memorial Faith. I knew the liturgy, the creeds and what they meant, the Catechism, the outward trappings of the faith of my ancestors. In religion class, I got the highest grade of my high school senior class; I even got a higher score than the girls, who always seemed to get higher grades than the boys. But right alongside that religious life, I lived another life—one that was self-absorbed, self-seeking, and self-indulgent. There was no inner faith in Christ. There was no deep longing to be close to Jesus. In high school, I lived for school activities, sports, and girlfriends. Because I was somewhat successful in all three, I felt a sense of worth by being involved in each. I went to church and religious instruction because it was what I was supposed to do and because I was given no choice in the matter.

College changed my religious behavior. I was no longer required to go to church on Sunday, so I no longer went. My night prayers became infrequent. I chose not to think about God or religion. Even though I attended a church-affiliated college, I worked hard to avoid situations where I had to address the question of my faith. In the exchange of ideas colleges are famous for, my Memorial Faith failed me. After a couple of conversations with fraternity brothers in which I tried to give a defense for my faith-belief system, I realized that I did not really believe in its defense. So I put my faith and energy into areas I knew would bring success—fraternity life, sports, and girlfriends. Having nothing with which to replace my failed Memorial Faith, I simply shut down that part of my life.

Much was happening on the international scene while I was in college. The first Roman Catholic President governed, giving me pride in my religious persuasion (even though I was not practicing it). John F. Kennedy confronted the Russians in Cuba and continued sending military advisers to Southeast Asia to assist in the containment of Communism there. Many in our country thought JFK was wonderful, and that he would lead us to victory in the Cold War. My grandparents had a picture of him on the wall of their kitchen, right next to the Pope.

I remember vividly the day President Kennedy was assassinated. I was out in the parking lot of my fraternity house fixing my 1947 Studebaker. Someone yelled out the door that Kennedy had been shot. Soon we were all gathered together around the television in the lounge taking in all the coverage of the assassination. As I think back on it, I realize how dead my Memorial Faith really was—I do not remember even once praying about that terrible event. The President was dead—so what now?

What now was a new president, and a whole new page in history—one that would threaten to run over me like a Mack truck. I had been in the Reserve Officers Training Corps (ROTC) since my freshman year. Although I did not particularly like ROTC, I stayed with it from 1961 to 1964 because I was interested in the helicopter pilot program. In my third year of college, my eyesight slipped below 20/20 and I was told I could not become a pilot. My interest in ROTC suddenly dropped to zero. Being immature and rebellious, I began to slip in performance expectations. I let my hair grow too long for Army standards, and was given demerits for not conforming. I also became sporadic in showing up for the required once-a-week military drills— more demerits. Toward the end of the year, the professor of Military Science called me into his office and explained that I had so many demerits that there was little chance I could work them all off before the end of the year. He therefore planned to give me the first "Failing Grade" in the history of ROTC at that institution. The only way I could avoid an "F," he said, was to work off the demerits by cleaning rifles every afternoon for the next four weeks! This proposal did not fit well with my daily routine. Several of us had gotten used to a sustained Happy Hour after class each day. So I gave a less than enthusiastic response to his proposition. I now realize, of course, that he was attempting to be charitable. I did not realize it then. After arguing with me for awhile, he finally gave up and told me that I was wasting my life, and that because of my bad attitude he would make sure that I never got into an officer program after college. He also explained that what I now faced was being drafted as soon as I finished college. In other words, he said, I was destined to become an Army Private! Outwardly I treated what he said as if I didn't care. Inwardly, I was scared that what he said would come true.

The following autumn, 1964, my senior year, the Marines hit the beach at Danang, Vietnam and the war was officially on. President Johnson brought the war out of the closet where several administrations before him had hidden it. While the Marines were hitting the beach in Vietnam, reality was hitting me in the face in Florida. Although I was training to be a public school teacher, I began to realize that I would never teach. The ROTC professor's reach was too long—I would not get a chance to teach school, because he would make sure I was drafted into the Army the day I graduated from college. I worried about that, but through it all I never thought about talking with God about it. I just sort of carried it in my mind, the way I carried a lot of unresolved conflicts. My solution in those days was that no problem was so big that it could not be drowned in gin.

One day while I was walking across the campus, I noticed a display table in the student union, with a Marine Captain standing beside it. I walked by and the captain asked if I was interested in becoming a Marine officer. Actually I had never thought about the Marines at all, much less about becoming one. I had never even met a Marine, as far as I could remember. My three older brothers had all been in the Navy, as had my father, and they told stories about the uncouth Marines they had met. Well, I reasoned, I was pretty uncouth, so why not listen to what this guy had to say.

The ROTC professor's reach evidently did not extend to the Marine Corps, because after taking the entrance exam, I was accepted into the Marine Officer Candidate Course, to begin active duty when I graduated from college. What I realize now is that God was quietly working in the circumstances of my life, moving through my immaturity to prepare me for a life's vocation.

The autumn of 1965 saw me rolling through the Marine Corps Officer Candidate Course at Quantico, Virginia. While there, I did manage to go to Mass every Sunday. The stress of being pushed beyond anything I had ever encountered sent me scurrying back to my childhood Memorial Faith for assurance and comfort. And gin was not available to solve my problems. So I attended the chapel services and prayed that I would survive the course and be commissioned. But in all that praying, I still did not sense a closeness with God. He was instead an insurance policy to get me through a tough time. And those three months of initial training were the toughest days I had experienced so far in my life. The training was frightening for me at first. I was dealing with one very mean Drill Instructor who was intent on weeding out everyone who could not take the pressure. But I soon found that I could do this "stuff!" It involved lots of athletic ability, learning how to march and conduct marches, clear reasoning, courage, and relatively easy academics. I finished as my platoon's honor graduate and was commissioned a Second Lieutenant.

Following commissioning, I entered the Basic School at Quantico. The Basic School was a six-month program that qualified us as infantry officers. Since the pressure of the Officer Candidate Course was over, I stopped attending church and again took up the drinking of gin. My self-confidence shot up, and my perceived need for God went down. I realize now that I had been using God as a crutch, but I did not realize it then.

I loved the Basic School and all it stood for. We got plenty of practice leading Marines in mock-combat, learned a lot about leadership, spent many days running through the beautiful hills of Virginia, and studied everything from world politics to basic first-aid. During this whole experience, my life changed dramatically. I moved from an immature, sometimes surly kid to a mature man. I learned about leadership, human dignity, and what it meant to be a responsible human being people could depend on. I also began to get in touch with the dangers of excessive use of alcohol, and began the long trek to sobriety. God would later use what I learned when He visited me with Miracle Faith.

A key element of the Basic School was deciding which officer specialty we would choose. Although we would all graduate as Infantry Officers, the majority of us would actually go into some other specialty. I was hoping to serve as an infantry platoon commander until I learned about the possibility of becoming a Naval flight officer. I had always wanted to fly, but because of my poor vision, had given up the hope of becoming a pilot. A Naval flight officer, I learned, was not a pilot, but was an officer who flew in a tactical aircraft as either a Radar Intercept Officer or as a bombardier/navigator. If one had no worse than 20/40 vision, one could apply. I squeaked by the vision exam, passed the aptitude test, and upon graduation from the Basic School, headed south to Naval Air Station Pensacola, Florida for aviation training.

It was at Pensacola that God did another thing in my life that was designed to move me in the direction He had in mind. He brought Mary Ellen into my life. Mary Ellen was a college student in Alabama, not far from Pensacola. It was a "God-incident" that brought us together, and it was love at first sight. Four Marines, myself included, had been renting a house on Pensacola Beach. While we worked hard in flight school during the week, partying was a huge part of every weekend, and the house on the beach drew a lot of women to us, none of which interested me in the long term. One of my leatherneck co-renters began dating an Alabama girl, who happened to be Mary Ellen's college roommate. She brought Mary Ellen to our house during Thanksgiving vacation, and upon meeting her it was all over for me! As we shared Thanksgiving dinner together, I fell deeply in love with her. It was not very long after we met that we both felt drawn to each other for a life-time. Upon completing flight school and receiving my wings as a Naval flight officer, I married Mary Ellen in a beautiful ceremony in the Navy Chapel in Washington D.C.

We moved into officer housing at Marine Corps Air Station Cherry Point, North Carolina and I began proficiency training as a member of All-Weather Attack Squadron 225, flying the new A-6 Intruder aircraft. The A-6 was an advanced, computer-laden bomber, designed to fly low to the ground in any weather and hit a target with-out the crew ever physically seeing it. The crew consisted of a pilot and a bombardier/naviga-tor. By close coordination, this crew could literally take an A-6 through mountain passes at low level without ever seeing the ground. The finely designed radar in the aircraft offered accurate "viewing" of the terrain, and the inertial navigation system and computer offered fairly reliable location updates. By flying low to the ground, the aircraft could slip below anti-aircraft radar, and thus attack targets previously impenetrable. I felt proud to have been selected to fly this aircraft, and I dove enthusiastically into the training at Cherry Point.

But something else began to happen to us, in addition to beginning married life on an active Marine base. We began attending church. Mary Ellen had a religious upbringing similar to mine, and had also pretty much dropped out of church in college. But while we were dating, during those romantic days when you talk about everything under and above the sun, we talked about our respective churches, and our faith. We decided that we should go to a church when we got married. Why we decided that, I don't know—the value of our parents faithfully taking us to church every Sunday when we were kids? Probably.

Whatever the reason, the important thing was that God got us back in church. Soon after we arrived at Cherry Point, we began attending a small Episcopal Church not far from our house. Since I had been brought up Roman Catholic and Mary Ellen had been brought up Protestant, we thought we could meet in the "middle," the Episcopal Church. An Episcopal chaplain had conducted our wedding ceremony, and he seemed like a good, faithful guy. Why not try the Episcopal Church?

As we got involved in the parish and became Episcopalians, Memorial Faith returned to my life. I learned about being an Episcopalian—Liturgy, Sacraments, Catechism, "Rules of the Religious Road." And I once again began saying my night prayers from childhood. I found that I could accommodate my Memorial Faith to membership in our new church without changing my slovenly lifestyle. No one at church ever spoke of personal faith. Prayers during worship were general in nature. Jesus Christ was mentioned each week in the Gospel Lesson, and the priest of the church, a good man, sometimes made excellent references to Jesus. But I did not hear anything that motivated me to move beyond ritualistic Memorial Faith. It is very possible that this Godly priest was preaching the life-changing Gospel to me, but I did not have ears to hear. I was too stuck in maintaining Memorial Faith by following ritualistic rules and speaking prayers of good form that did not affect my daily life.

One night at a parish potluck supper, we saw a movie about the preparation people go through to be ordained. As I watched the movie, I got the strangest idea—I would one day become a priest!

I learned much later, after reflecting on all that happened, that this was God's Miracle Faith in action. Just as He had used unusual circumstances in my life to move me toward the Marine

Corps and maturity, and had found an unusual place to provide a life-partner for me, He was now using a movie about seminary to nudge me in the next right direction. Miracle Faith! I didn't know what it all meant at the time, but I knew it was somehow very important. It is interesting to note that I was so immersed in the Memorial Faith of my childhood that I did not even recognize what this amazing shift of present tense faith was until it smacked me in the face.

I mentioned the idea of becoming a priest to Mary Ellen when we got home that night. She was frightened by it. She said she had married a Marine, not a preacher; she wasn't sure she could deal with that big of a change in our lives. But the idea wouldn't go away, hard as I tried to erase it from my mind. We continued our involvement in church, joined the choir, attended potluck dinners, and helped with the Stewardship Campaign. But we tried not to talk about this new possibility. It was just too confusing. I was flying at all hours of the night and day, preparing for my tour in Vietnam. Mary Ellen was pregnant. We had enough on our plate without adding the dilemma of whether or not to go to seminary. But soon an enormous change would take place in my faith. I would move into a new stage.

Chapter Three

Memories
Are Made of This

Troubled in My Soul

After nine months at Cherry Point, I received orders to report for duty in Vietnam. Mary Ellen and I had known from the beginning I would have to go to war, so we were not surprised when my name came up for a thirteen month combat tour. We decided that during the thirteen-month separation, I would figure out what this whole religion thing meant for my life and for our marriage. I thought the war might provide a good backdrop for my examination of faith and ministry. I also had some excitement in my soul about going to war and making a difference for America by my participation as an American fighting man.

Just before I left for Vietnam, I received word that my college roommate, a fellow Marine, had just crashed his helicopter while on a rescue mission in Vietnam, and was in critical condition in a California hospital. Since I had to go through California, I decided to stop by the hospital to see him. What I found in that hospital room was a badly burned, very sick friend. Brownie tried to talk to me but he was so badly wounded his words came with great difficulty. In the first two minutes of my visit with him, my whole romanticized view of war changed. If this was what war did, what was I getting myself into? That night, I was deeply troubled in my soul. I was on my way to war—I could wind up like Brownie. I tried to pray, but the words would not come. After struggling with this new realization most of the night, I finally tucked it deeply into the back of my mind and refused to consciously deal with it.

I reported to Chu Lai Air Base, Vietnam, in early April 1968, leaving behind a very pregnant and beautiful young wife. It was hard saying goodbye. I was now a captain and a qualified bombardier/navigator, and joined All-Weather Attack Squadron 533, the "Night Hawks." After a few days of orientation, I began flying bombing missions over North Vietnam. Our mission was to take off from Chu Lai, fly at high altitude north just off the North Vietnamese coast, and then descend to low-level for penetration into the landmass of North Vietnam. Once over land, we would search out and destroy enemy truck convoys carrying ammunition and supplies south from Hanoi/Haiphong to the North Vietnamese and Vietcong troops in South Vietnam. On my first mission north, we encountered unbelievable anti-aircraft fire. It was like flying through the middle of a fireworks display. But I knew that these fireworks were deadly bullets aimed at tearing our aircraft apart! I wanted to throw up, both from the updrafts that bounced our aircraft around like a basketball, and from the fear of being shot down. The fear was incredible. Somehow we managed to drop our bombs on several convoys, and return to Chu Lai without sustaining battle damage. I remember walking off the flight line that night thinking, "No way can I go through thirteen months of this!"

So it was extremely difficult for me to climb back into that A-6 the next night and again become a "sitting duck" for the North Vietnamese gunners. Everything in me was shouting, "Call in sick!" But I could find no reason not to fly, so fly I did. We returned safely the second night after again flying through anti-aircraft fire. And the next night, and the next. In fact, I landed safely more than 250 times in thirteen months, and came back only twice with battle damage to our aircraft.

But during that first month of the nightly bombing raids, I was keenly aware that I might not return safely, and so I began to take my post-life destination more seriously. Prior to this time, I had addressed the afterlife only from a philosophical point of view. Was there really a hell or was it a concept church and society used to motivate civilized behavior? Was there really a heaven or was it just a hope of human beings who could not face the possibility that their life would really end when they died? What did the theologians say about the God-human encounter? Would it be hell or would it be purgatory and eventually heaven? Was purgatory a reality or was it simply a convenient concept to help us deal with our guilt?

It is one thing to intellectualize the afterlife from a safe classroom environment. It is another to deal with it up-close. In combat, the afterlife took on a new significance for me. I found I could give no credibility to professors writing stuffy books, professors whose only encounter with danger was an occasional angry student who couldn't deal with a low grade. On the second night after my arrival in Vietnam, two of my squadron mates were killed in combat.

And if flying dangerous bombing missions each night was not enough, I also had to contend with mortar and rocket attacks. Chu Lai Air Base was regularly rocketed by the enemy. Many nights saw me running into the bunker as mortar and rocket rounds went off around me. Bottom line? There was now a nightly opportunity for me to face my Maker in death! What would it be for me if I got blown out of the sky? Or if a mortar round came crashing into my hut before I could head for the bunker? And coming back to my consciousness on a regular basis was the memory of my friend Brownie struggling for life in that hospital back in California. Sometimes I imagined myself lying there in his place. Sometimes, I felt I should be the one lying there rather than Brownie. After all, I had encouraged him to join the Marines after I had joined. "Survivor's guilt" began doing a job on my head, my heart, and my soul. I began to really think about what my purpose in life was, and what my future might be.

Keeping to my agreement with Mary Ellen, I also began exploring the call I was feeling to ordained ministry. I started attending the weekly chapel services, and became friends with some of the guys who attended regularly. Even though several of our comrades had already died or disappeared in the war, none of us who attended chapel talked about the possibility that death might actually happen to us. I wished we would talk about it, but I was not about to be the one who brought it up. Nobody seemed to be the one to bring it up. Even the chaplain, who preached great sermons, did not bring up the afterlife in a way that answered any of my questions. I began to look for any group that might address the issue.

One Sunday the chaplain announced that there would be a Bible study and discussion session starting on Tuesday nights. I attended these sessions, which were led by one of my squadron mates. Finally, I was able to find answers to my questions.

As we looked through the Holy Scriptures together, things began to fall into place for me. You see, I had never really studied the Bible before—never even owned one. My friend gave me a Bible, and shared with me what it said about God's love for me. I found out that God wants to have a close relationship with all of His people. But my sin and rebelliousness had been causing a continuing and eternal rift between God and me. That's why God sent His Incarnate Son Jesus into the world. Jesus shows us what God is really like. He teaches us how to love as responsible humans. While I did not understand how it all worked, I accepted the biblical truth that Jesus took my sins to the cross and dealt with their eternal consequences. In fact, God dealt with my problem concerning an afterlife: Jesus defeated death in order for me to live eternally with Him in heaven. As my friend and I went through the Bible, he showed me passage after passage of God's deep love for me. I began to realize that this was not a God who was angry with me or who wanted to send me to hell. This was a God who loved me in a profound and wonderful way.

For the first time, it all began to make sense. And it was all right there in the Bible waiting for me to discover God's Truth. Led by my friend, I acknowledged my sin, repented of it, and invited Jesus Christ to enter my life as Lord and Savior. To my surprise, I found this change of faith perspective a life-changing encounter! What a difference it is to trust God rather than fear Him!

I don't want you to think that from that day on, everything was perfect for me. In the months that followed, I talked for hours at a time with my pilot, Bill, about my new found faith journey, as well as the doubts that dogged me. Bill was not a believer at the time, and his critical feedback of my journey was important to me. Ten years older and more mature, he seemed to be able to ask just the right question at the right time to make me think hard about what it meant to live the Christian life on a daily basis. Even though he did not believe as I did, he wanted what was best for me. And so, when we were not flying, he acted as a critical tutor—congratulating me when what I said made sense, and bringing me back to reality when I was "out to lunch."

Under Bill's tutelage, and as a result of the serious Bible studies I was attending, my spiritual and prayer life began to grow. And I was reading every book on faith I could get my hands on. Of particular help was Keith Miller's *The Taste of New Wine*. Keith felt what I felt; experienced what I experienced; had the same doubts I had. I read and reread his "aha moment" when he pulled his car over to the side of a dusty Texas road and in effect said, "OK, Lord. I'm giving you my life. If you can do anything with this stinking body, have at it." I had said almost the same thing only days before! I consumed Keith's book like a starving man eating bread. And I was spiritually strengthened by it.

Slowly I began to realize that the reason for living a virtuous life had nothing to do with avoiding hell. Its purpose was instead a way of loving God, a God who longed to see me at peace within myself and with fellow human beings. Peace came to dominate my life as I began a daily conversation with Jesus Christ, read the Bible each day, and tried to pattern my life after what I read about Jesus. My new life had begun. I spent my days praising God, spending time reading the Bible, and trying to clean up my act. In our weekly Bible study group, we dealt with the afterlife, with the Just War Doctrine and our part in prosecuting the war, and with living a whole-some lifestyle in the midst of dropping bombs. I was growing spiritually! My conversion, which began in late April 1968, became a benchmark time in my life. It marked the time I was born anew into eternal life!

Of course, I had to live out my combat tour, which included those 252 bombing missions, numerous rocket and mortar attacks by the North Vietnamese on our air base, the loss of several more friends in combat, and over a year of sepa-ration from my wife and new daughter. During that tour, however, I read everything I could get my hands on regarding spiritual development, and attended Bible studies and prayer groups. As a result, I grew in my knowledge of the Bible and felt an increasing closeness with the person of Jesus Christ.

I also got in touch with the whole question of becoming an ordained person. I discerned that God wanted me to become a chaplain to the Armed Forces—to help others who like myself were struggling with the age-old questions of life and death.

The Big Move—
From Memorial to Memory Faith

What you have just read is an example of what many have gone through in a conversion experience. This experience moved me from an inherited Memorial Faith to a fresh Memory Faith. My friend called what happened to me a "born again" experience. But at the time I didn't care what it was called. It was wonderful! My faith now was based on an experience with God. Still within me was Memorial Faith, but that faith became latent. I had now developed my own relationship with God, a relationship based on a faith experience. This Memory Faith would serve me well in the days that followed.

I came home from the war and spent another year flying for the Marines as I went through preparations for seminary. We went back to the Cherry Point Marine Corps Air Station in North Carolina and again got involved with our church. But it was different this time. I was deeply drawn into the faith development of others. Mary Ellen and I became youth group advisors. I became a lay reader and began preaching lay sermons. I continually engaged other Marines in talks about the God revealed in Jesus Christ. The main thing I talked about was my conversion in April of

1968. I was deeply into Memory Faith, basing everything on my own "born again" experience, and trying to get others to be born again.

Eventually my priest took me to see the bishop about entering seminary. Being a former Marine himself, the bishop was excited about ordained ministry for me, and put me on the fast track for seminary. A year and a half after returning from combat, we moved to Virginia where I started three years of seminary training. Seminary was easy for me in some ways and difficult in others. The academics were relatively easy. I was organized, able to read quickly, and did well on examinations and research papers. I also enjoyed the internships. I loved ministry, and enjoyed caring for people in parishes, hospitals, and nursing homes. I was able to share my born again experience with others, and was able to help a number of people into a deeper relationship with Jesus Christ.

But there were difficulties as well. Before entering seminary, I had imagined that life there would be blissful, with everyone spending hours together enjoying Bible study and prayer groups. Life at seminary proved not to be like that at all! While the faculty members were Godly people intent on preparing us for ordained ministry, the student body was made up of people of all sorts and conditions. Some, I judged, loved the Lord as I did, and wanted to learn how to communicate the Gospel to an unbelieving world. But others, I judged, were not at all sure what faith was all about. Some were just out of college and still very immature when it came to alcohol and drug use. And some deep thinkers thought that faith was much more complicated than I wanted to make it. They thought my born again experience was very simplistic and definitely "un-Episcopalian." One fellow seminarian told me, "Why are you in an Episcopal seminary? You ought to be a Baptist. They're the ones who talk about a personal deal with Jesus. Both you and we would be a lot happier if you transferred out of here!"

And I realized that some students were there so that they would not have to go into the military. They had military deferments! I judged, probably accurately, that they were extremely uncomfortable having a decorated war veteran in their midst—they felt that being a religious person and engaging in war were incompatible values. Wow. There were days in seminary when I thought that being in the war had been less stressful than being a seminarian.

I struggled through the three academic years, bouncing between feelings of self-righteousness over the slovenly lifestyles of some of my classmates, and feelings of guilt brought on by classmates who told me that I had committed murder in the war. I had to realize that shortly after accepting Christ, I had experienced conflicted feelings regarding dropping bombs on people and killing them. I swung from having a careless attitude about where my bombs fell to a fear that I might miss the enemy truck convoys and hit helpless civilians instead. Then I spent several bombing missions "missing" the targets altogether, and dumping our bombs where they would hit no one—rice paddies. My pilot Bill had grown a bit suspicious about my sudden lack of accuracy, and eventually forced me to think through the implications of representing my country in a war. He was immensely helpful in getting me to define just what I believed about one country using controlled violence against another country in order to bring good out of evil, as St. Augustine wrote. But still the feelings lingered.

Through some good Christian counseling in seminary, I was finally able to lay these conflicted feelings to rest. And when all else failed, I would fall back on Memory Faith, the experience that had changed my life. "I have been saved by God's grace through faith in Jesus Christ," I would say to myself, "The date was April 23, 1968. Nothing anyone says can take that away from me!"

But while I had experienced an authentic conversion experience with God, and that in itself seemed miraculous, I still had not experienced Miracle Faith. Seminary provided me the opportunity to learn much about the Church and its ministry. But my faith development seemed to go nowhere during that three-year period. I had opened the door for God to enter in, but I had not opened it very far.

Chapter Four

You Like
Roller Coasters?

A Move Into Miracle Faith

Following seminary, we moved back to North Carolina, where I served as the Assistant Rector of a large, downtown parish. I pretty much operated on Memory Faith there, inviting people to make decisions to follow Christ. This was an effective ministry, and I am sure I led a number of people into a deeper relationship with Jesus Christ. But I still felt uncomfortable about my faith development. I just didn't see any progress toward closeness with God. Working for a kindly rector who had been in combat in World War II—and thus understood where I was coming from—I was enabled to begin looking beyond Memory Faith. Was there something else God had in mind for me? I began to stretch my faith boundaries.

After serving two years in North Carolina, I realized that God had something else for me to do. Since there were no openings for chaplains in the armed forces due to the Vietnam draw-down, and since I loved parish ministry, I became open to a new parish assignment. Eventually I accepted a call to a large parish in Texas, this time a parish in the midst of spiritual renewal. I took a position as the Associate Rector, giving me more responsibility for the day-to-day life of the parish. Once again I was blessed with a faithful rector who, in supervising me, also helped me stretch beyond Memory Faith. Because the parish was in the beginning of a process of physically moving to a more visible location, the rector was deeply involved in plans for the move. Thus he allowed me much latitude in managing the day-to-day life of the congregation. It was here that another cataclysmic experience changed my life. It was at this point that I realized that I was approaching something very big, almost fearful!

By now, Mary Ellen and I had been married eight years and had two small children. The incredible pressure of ministering to over a thousand parishioners, developing and pushing programs for people of all ages, and all the time trying to be a good husband and father began to weigh heavily upon me. To add to the pressure, I still had a goal of returning to active military service as a chaplain, a goal that was being blocked by the post-war drawdown in personnel. The armed services were not interested in hiring; they were interested in firing. I felt frustrated that my prayers for an opening in the chaplaincy were not being answered in the way I wished.

While I found parish life in Austin to be extremely exciting and enjoyable, I also began to experience burnout, disillusionment, and frustration. For the first time, I found that Memory Faith was not enough all by itself! I began to realize that God had not meant for me to base my faith on a once-in-a-lifetime experience. God used heavy-duty parish ministry to bring me to the point of really addressing faith from a new perspective. Up to this point, I had done quite well operating out of my own talents and work ethic. The lessons learned from being a Marine officer had been a tool God had given me for effective ministry. But I somehow had missed the other lesson—*allowing the power of God to guide and empower my ministry*. So I now was in over my head. Hard as I tried, I could not effectively minister to my family, and still be able to work 70-hour weeks ministering in the parish. I felt my marriage becoming strained because of the long hours I worked. The harder I tried to carry both loads, the more frustrating life became.

One day when I was on the way to visit a parishioner in the hospital, I got stuck in a traffic jam. Going nowhere fast, I began to think about life in general, and all that I was trying to cope with. Anxiety and depression flooded through me.

"I give up, Lord!" I muttered. "I can't do this anymore! It's just too hard. I'm caught in a *life* traffic jam here, and I am going nowhere fast! Come in and rearrange my life."

That moment was the beginning of Miracle Faith. To quote an old maxim—"man's extremity becomes God's opportunity." As I sat there in the traffic, I thought about my marriage. Some changes had to be made soon in that department! Mary Ellen and I were having a difficult time relating to each other. So much had happened to us in such a short period of time—a separation while I went off to war, bearing two kids in short order, a change in occupation, several moves! I discovered that in trying to compensate for the swift changes in our life, I was using some destructive tactics to have our relationship on what I thought were safe terms—mine. I was over-controlling our marriage life, and when things didn't go the way I thought they should, I would play the martyr. This was a difficult time for Mary Ellen and me, as we tried to figure out how to have a more fulfilling relationship.

And some changes had to happen soon in my work. I was working way too many hours, and couldn't seem to knock off for the day at a decent hour. There were morning worship services and meetings, afternoon visitations and meetings, evening study groups and meetings! Saturdays brought youth activities and meetings! Sunday? Forget about it! How was I going to defeat the workaholic monster that was chasing me? As I sat there in that traffic jam, God began to show me areas that needed "spiritual surgery." And the surgery was going to start very soon!

A few months prior to the traffic jam, my brother and sister-in-law had suggested we try an Episcopal Marriage Encounter Weekend. Reluctantly we signed up for one in Houston, found a sitter for the kids, and went.

Wow! That turned out to be God's Weekend for us! During the forty-four hours of that crash course in Christian marriage, we began to learn the language of couple communication. A new romance entered our marriage as we learned to lovingly work out our feelings about all that had happened to us. And we developed a whole new vision of God in our marriage. We began praying together, and joined a continuing Marriage Encounter group whose whole purpose was to encourage growth in couple relationships.

As we *together* became more involved with people through parish Bible study and prayer groups, we learned a new thing from these wonderful people—a new kind of personal power that God offers each of us; a power that brought tears to my eyes as I felt a freshness in our marriage relationship! Mary Ellen and I began to realize that in reading the story of Jesus, God's Spirit was coming into our life and marriage relationship. We could feel His presence and warmth. It felt good to spend more time together—walking, talking, dating. And it felt good to spend playtime with the kids!

As for me, I realized that God had to be the Head of our family. What a relief! I gave Him permission to be the Head of our little family. It was with a feeling of assurance that I followed His lead by cutting back on my burdensome work hours in order to nurture this family He had made me a part of.

The second thing that brought a sense of immediacy about faith into my life was my relationship with the men of the parish. Several of the more mature men spoke to me of "letting go and letting God." Their lives told me they knew how to do this, so I sought guidance from them. One good ol' Texan gave me sage advice— "Just do it, David! Invite God's Holy Spirit to take over the management of your business, and of your life! Just say it like you mean it—simple and clear. And then believe into it!"

I did, and God did. My life came under new management. I no longer had to control everything. I just had to give it to God and then show up!

This is how I learned about what people mean when they talk of being filled with the power of the Holy Spirit. *You can do it on your own strength and feel exhausted; or you can do it in the power of the Holy Spirit and feel exhilarated!* That's what I learned. I can turn it all over to New Management.

I learned that I did not need to do everything in the parish that was asked of me. By planning out the week asking, "OK, Lord, what are we going to do this week?" I learned that a lot of things I was showing up for did not really require my attendance. I began to get in touch with the principle that it was better to train someone to do a certain ministry than for me to keep doing it myself. Miracles began to happen! I was working fewer hours but getting more done! Sermons became more alive, filled with stories, and fun, both to prepare and to share. Everyday, by letting the Real Leader guide me, I began to feel more at home as a parish leader. Both family life and ordained life became exciting and new. I said to myself, "Maybe that's what humility's about—seeing life and myself honestly."

One day I was sitting in my office looking out the window at the beautiful Austin skyline, and it came to me: "My faith is not a memory anymore! God, you are right here with me, guiding me as I live out a whole new experience!" I discovered what I am calling in this book Miracle Faith. It was truly a blessed time in my life. And then I found out what God was preparing me for.

Just as I was getting totally comfortable with ministry in that wonderful Texas parish, my name finally came out on the list for active duty military service. Go figure! I guess God wanted me to be more nearly His before He affirmatively answered my prayers for chaplain service.

And so I entered service as an Air Force chaplain. As I look back on it, I now see that I needed Miracle Faith to serve as a chaplain in the very difficult settings of military service. In addition to serving military congregations, I also ministered to troops of all faith traditions and some with no faith at all. I ministered in hot, dry deserts, and on the cold, snow-covered tundra. I conducted worship services from a jeep for young airmen in the field and I conducted worship services in the Pentagon for high-ranking officers. And all the while, I opened myself to the Holy Spirit so that I could be God's instrument of healing and wholeness to people in difficult and dangerous situations.

Because I ministered alongside chaplains of a number of denominations, and in an ecumenical environment, I was able to see "the good, the bad, and the ugly" of the various denominational groups, including my own. I learned how people of some faith groups box a living presence of God out of their churches by being too protective of their traditions. And I learned how people of some faith groups open their churches to God by staying close to Jesus Christ, the Lord of Life, in spite of their traditions. My life opened more to a consciousness of the presence of God as I learned from others!

My old Memorial Faith came back, but not as a sterile tradition. Instead, it took on a renewed and deeper meaning for me. I learned to prize the great traditions of my Church without living in the past. And my old Memory Faith also came back, but not as a distant experience. I realized the truth that until one is in a close, personal relationship with Jesus, faith will have a hollowness to it. Having a life-changing experience with Christ is a great gift. It creates a specific memory of one's own experience that can be drawn on when the going gets tough—Memory Faith. And Memory Faith can make Memorial Faith come alive! Ritual is rich with meaning when it is experienced with a converted heart; the ancient traditions of the Church Catholic take on a whole new significance when one comes at them from a close relationship with Jesus.

But most of all, I learned the importance of Miracle Faith—placing all I am and all I have under the power of the Holy Spirit, God present—and then moving into the miracle of life with Jesus walking beside me. In sum, as I began to live into the gift of Miracle Faith, the Lord eventually gave me the gift of seeing the positive aspects of Memorial Faith and of Memory Faith as well—three gifts for eternity!

After many years in the Air Force, I retired and became the Executive Assistant to the Episcopal Bishop for the Armed Forces. Here I learned about ministering on the diocesan level. My job was akin to being the Canon to the Ordinary for a diocesan bishop—assisting the bishop in whatever way he desired, recruiting new chaplains, dealing with people issues, developing continuing education programs for clergy, helping in the whole area of clergy discipline. Working together closely, the bishop and I were able to effectively support Episcopal chaplains of the Armed Forces, Veterans Administration, and Federal Prisons in their faith development and ministries.

As God would have it, I then received a call to a parish in upstate New York, only ten miles from where I was born! That in itself was a miracle. And Mary Ellen and I dove gleefully into the wonderful waters of Calvary Church, Burnt Hills, where I spent over five joy-filled years as rector. Those five and a half years were the happiest of our life so far. Together, Mary Ellen and I placed ourselves under the power of the Holy Spirit, and utilized our years of pastoral experience to help bring the parish into spiritual renewal. One of the best jobs one can have is that of parish priest, *when* one allows the Holy Spirit to run the operation and highlight Jesus as Head of the Church.

And then I was elected by my diocese to be the Suffragan Bishop. In this position, I am *really* learning about Miracle Faith! While we have some very dynamic and exciting congregations in our diocese, many of our parishes are patched together with "bailing wire and chewing gum." We have many retirement-aged clergy ("Thank you, Lord, for active retired clergy") faithfully ministering as best they can in parishes where the townspeople have mostly fled to the Sunbelt. We have aging parishioners who can't seem to figure out how to get younger people involved. We have dwindling numbers in our Sunday schools. And we have a number of people who don't know how to express their Christian faith in words, or who seem uncomfortable with talking about God. The fact that the Church even continues seems like a miracle in itself! I see good people, trying very hard to be Christian, keeping churches open when the odds say otherwise.

Although we are seeing promising trends in spiritual vitality and attendance, we still have a long way to go as we allow the Holy Spirit to work through us. And so I move along, preaching and teaching in the parishes of our diocese, trying to "guard the faith, unity, and discipline of the Church; to celebrate and to provide for the administration of the sacraments of the New Covenant; to ordain priests and deacons and to join in ordaining bishops; and to be in all things a faithful pastor and wholesome example for the entire flock of Christ" (from "The Ordination of a Bishop"—The Book of Common Prayer, page 517).

And so this book: a bishop teaching the Christian faith; seeking to inspire people to proclaim the transforming Gospel of Jesus Christ in season and out, in the city and in the country; helping people integrate Memorial Faith and Memory Faith into the beauty of Miracle Faith. May God bless you as you go through these pages. May you grow in your love for God, your fellow sojourners, yourself, and your environment.

Now you've heard my faith story. If you can identify with anything about my struggles or what I've gone through, you might be interested in some insights I've picked up about an authentic Christian faith—Memorial Faith, Memory Faith, and Miracle Faith.

Section Two

The Good, Bad, and Ugly of Memorial Faith

Chapter Five

Here's the Good Stuff!

Let's Start the Journey Together

This book is geared toward helping us discover the beauty of Miracle Faith—to go through the valley of Memorial Faith and come out on the beautiful mountain of miraculous faith. Memorial Faith is not just a valley, however. It has many good points. This chapter will examine the wonder of Memorial Faith. Let's start that journey together, asking the Holy Spirit to be our guide.

Some time ago, I had a friend I'll call Ralph. Ralph and I served together in a Marine attack squadron in Vietnam. We were both bombardier/navigators with A-6 Intruder aircraft. We both trained in the same squadron in the states before going to Vietnam, and we both attended the same church there. Ralph was the kind of guy everyone admired—dedicated, friendly, faithful. He was a family man who loved his wife and little girl, and though still in his twenties, was proving to be an effective church leader. I liked Ralph a lot, and respected him for his faithful stand for Christ. Everyone respected him, whether they were churchgoers or not.

One night in 1969, Ralph and his pilot took off at midnight from Chu Lai Air Base, Vietnam on a bombing mission into Laos to attack an enemy truck convoy carrying weapons and ammunition down the Ho Chi Minh Trail bound for the Vietcong. Ralph's aircraft encountered intense flak and bad weather. They were flying an aircraft with a degraded avionics system that failed to give reliable information on the enemy anti-aircraft threat. After conducting several nightmarish attacks on the convoy, and dropping most of their bombs on the enemy trucks, the crew had just six bombs left and decided to make one final pass. Somehow they got confused on that last pass. Ralph and his pilot literally flew into the side of a nearby mountain. After the crash, they never came up on their emergency radios. They simply vanished. The American rescue teams went in the next day but found nothing, not even the remains of the aircraft. Suspecting that they were dead but having no evidence to prove it, the American Command declared them missing in action. Four years later when the American Prisoners of War were freed and Ralph was not among them, he was declared killed in action. His remains were finally found in 1999, thirty years after he died in the war.

Every Memorial Day since 1974 when Ralph was declared "Killed in Action," I have thought of him and the sacrifice he and other friends of mine made for their country. Whether or not the Vietnam War was justified, these men and women answered the call of our nation to defend it and they gave up their lives doing so. I think about all those people who died at a young age doing for the United States what they thought was the honorable thing to do. They should be honored for that. Memorial Day in America is a day to remember those who in all wars and conflicts gave up their lives for the rest of us. They sacrificed so that we might be free.

Now let's change the scene, and focus on our faith in God. Sometimes our faith is a lot like Memorial Day. Is that the way your Christian faith is—simply a way of remembering that Jesus died to protect our Christian freedom? Or is your faith a miraculous faith, a day-to-day relationship with Jesus? My contention is that, left to our own devices, we allow our faith to become simply a memorial to a good God, a formal and ritualistic way of honoring God. When that happens our faith does not develop fully. It never reaches the beautiful, recreative relationship God intends it to be. It becomes instead the equivalent of a stone memorial—recalling to us God's great sacrifice, but devoid of present day reality. You know what? Our faith does not have to be that way!

Let's look at the Scriptures to see the good points of Memorial Faith. But before we hit the road with Joshua and the miraculous crossing of the Jordan River, let's focus on the word *memorial*. A memorial can be many things. It can be an annual gathering to honor the memory of a person or event. Memorial Day is one of those gatherings, played out nationwide with services in cemeteries and parks.

Sometimes people will gather annually to remember the life of a particular person. We all know about the annual, almost cultic event in Memphis where people gather to remember Elvis Presley, or in New York's Central Park to remember the shooting of John Lennon of Beatles fame.

Looked at from another perspective, a memorial can be a gift given in the name of someone who has died. Churches are filled with memorials to departed loved ones—stained glass windows, Communion metalware, books, even musical instruments. I once had to turn down a request from someone who wanted to donate a stone statute of her dog! In the secular world it has become popular to line a particular location with loads of flowers as a memorial to a loved one or a celebrity. Remember watching Princess Diana's funeral on television and seeing all the flowers the common people had strewn by the gate to the palace? The gift of all those flowers was a way of saying, "This person meant a lot to us. We are thankful she passed this way. This is our memorial to her."

A memorial can also be a stone monument that reminds us of an event. City parks are full of stone monuments of wars fought, engraved with the names of people from that community who died in those wars.

There's the old joke of the family, with little boy in tow, who came to church on a Sunday morning. On the way out of the church, the boy noticed the Memorial Plaque honoring sons and daughters of that parish who had given the ultimate sacrifice for their country. The little boy asked his mother, "Mom, what is that stone thing?" Mom replied, "Son, that's a memorial honoring the people of this parish that died in the service." To which the boy shrieked, "Wow! Was it the 8 or the 10 o'clock service?"

If you get the opportunity, visit the Vietnam Memorial in Washington, D.C. It is a bewildering and sobering feeling to walk along a wall in which are engraved the names of the 58,000 Americans who died in that terrible conflict. Close to the wall, there are several sculptures representing the men and women who served in Vietnam. The sculptor does a fine job of showing that all races and both genders of

Americans served there. The other significant thing the sculptor showed—they all look like teenagers! It is sobering to spend contemplative time wandering around the Vietnam Memorial. It causes me to contemplate what life on the planet would be like if we were able to do away with wars. Sometimes a nation has no choice but to go to war, and a sense of fulfillment comes to the people of the nation when they have defeated the nation at fault. And often nations jump precipitously into war before exhausting peaceful solutions. But whether the war be just or unjust, it is our young who pay the ultimate price.

Point: Memorials can be effective instruments in forming and galvanizing a people! They can also cause us to stop and ponder the deeper issues of life.

Armed with this perspective on memorials, let's take a look at a significant event in the life of the nation of Israel during biblical times, an event that was memorialized.

Crossing the River Without a Bridge!

So let's jump into the Bible and find some Memorial Faith—Joshua and the miraculous crossing of the Jordan River.

*Joshua said, "Behold, the ark of the cov-
enant of the Lord of all the earth is to pass
over before you into the Jordan River..." So,
when the people set out from their tents, to
pass over the Jordan with the priests bearing
the ark of the covenant before the people, and
when those who bore the ark had come to the
Jordan, and the feet of the priests bearing the
ark were dipped in the brink of the water (the
Jordan overflows all its banks throughout the
time of harvest), the waters coming down from
above stood and rose up in a heap far off...
and the people passed over opposite Jericho.
And while all Israel were passing over on dry
ground, the priests who bore the ark of the
covenant of the Lord stood on dry ground in
the midst of the Jordan, until all the nation
finished passing over the Jordan.*

Joshua 3:11, 14-17
—Revised Standard Version

Can you imagine that? We have all heard that
Moses had his miraculous Red Sea crossing, but
few of us know about Joshua's Jordan River
crossing—every bit as spectacular! The author
tries to help us into the excitement of the crossing by informing us that this was harvest season
when the river traditionally burst its banks—it

was not some trickle of water they crossed!

Moses had by now died, leaving Joshua to bring the people of Israel, thousands upon thousands of them, into the Promised Land. Under Moses' leadership, they had turned what should have been a week's journey to the Promised Land into a miserable forty-year trip in the wilderness. It ended up taking them forty years because they were a very obstinate people intent on having this new nation *their* way instead of God's. They kicked and bucked most of the way, so it took a long time for them to get broken enough to follow God's guidance. During this forty-year period, God also worked with them, transforming them from a disorganized slave people into an effective nation and powerful military force. Now, after forty long years they were poised to actually cross the Jordan River and take possession of the "Land of Milk and Honey." But how would they cross, especially at a time of the year when the river was bursting its banks? This was not the age of floating heavy cranes, pontoon bridges, ferryboats, or concrete abutments.

Most armies crossed rivers at shallow areas known as fords. And they had to wait on the weather—when the water was low, they crossed. Joshua did not have the luxury of waiting. He needed a miracle to get his troops across the

Jordan! He followed God's directions to the letter with confidence that God would come through.

God delivered! The river somehow got dammed north of the crossing, and ran right into the Dead Sea on the south side, leaving a dry path across what had been a raging river. You figure it out! Many scholars have come up with natural phenomena to explain this miracle. So maybe God used natural phenomena to perform the miracle! But He did it in His timing and in His way. That's the miracle!

Not only did the Israelites experience the miraculous crossing, but the enemy, the Canaanites, also saw the miracle take place. Who were the Canaanites? They were the then occupants of the Promised Land, the tenants who were idolatrous, polytheistic, hedonistic people and in general not very excited about giving up their land to these Holier-Than-Thou-Johnny-Come-Latelys. The Canaanites knew the Israelites were heading for them. They knew a war was inevitable. They were dressed for war, but figured they had some months to really get ready because it would take that long for the Israelites to figure out where and when to cross the Jordan. Imagine their surprise when they saw the Israelite Army walking across the river on dry land! When the Canaanites saw the miracle, their courage melted, faded, and abated! This gave God the opportunity to get two outcomes for the price of one miracle: (1) The Israelites got across the Jordan, and (2) watching the miraculous crossing, the Canaanites were defeated before the battle even started. And defeated they were, as the Israelites spent the next several years vanquishing them one battle at a time, until Israel had regained the ancient ancestral lands God had promised them.

After experiencing the miraculous crossing and seeing the wonderful effect it had on his nation, Joshua foresaw its usefulness for motivating future generations of Israelites. Joshua swung into action. He knew the power of Memorial Faith. He knew that it would galvanize his people into a force capable of completing the job God had given them.

> *Then Joshua called the twelve men from the people of Israel whom he had appointed, a man from each tribe; and Joshua said to them, "Pass on before the ark of the Lord your God into the midst of the Jordan, and take up each of you a stone upon his shoulder, according to the numbering of tribes of the people of Israel, that this may be a sign among you,*

*when your children ask in time to come, 'What
do those stones mean to you?' then you shall
tell them that the waters of the Jordan were
cut off before the ark of the covenant of the
Lord; when it passed over the Jordan, the
waters of the Jordan were cut off. So these
stones shall be to the people of Israel a memorial for ever."* Joshua 4:4-7

Do you see what a genius Joshua was, with a
little help from God? God had wrought a miracle
so that the people of Israel could go in and claim
the Promised Land. Joshua knew that the effects
of miracles can be short-lived if they are not
memorialized. Joshua had to have a way to keep
his troops motivated for the years it would take
to claim all the land. So he had the miraculous
crossing memorialized—a stone monument! That
rock memorial could be returned to again and
again to remind the Israelites that God was their
protector. In this case, people could go back for
years to that site near Jericho on the Jordan, look
at that great pile of twelve rocks and hear the
story again of how God delivered the people
across the river by drying up the bed for them.

"Do you see these great rocks? Our fathers
carried them right out of the middle of the
Jordan in the midst of flood season! Our God is

powerful enough to dam the mighty Jordan for us. We can trust Him to carry us to victory." Can't you hear the parents passing the family / national history on to their children, thus inspiring yet another generation? Can't you just see little ten-year-olds in their neighborhoods playing the game of God halting the Jordan, some pretending to be priests carrying the ark into the river, others pretending that they were the troops lumbering across the mud with their military gear and finally finding rocks to build the monument "just like the one down on the Jordan?"

Memorials can do that! They can galvanize a people. They can teach and inspire a nation.

The Advantage of a Memorial Faith for You and Me

The Israelites spent a whole Bible memorializing the stories of God's providential care. Christians have continued that tradition. Our faith is strong today because we have been steeped in the stories of God's victory and power. One reason we have crosses in our churches, around our necks, on our walls, and on top of our sacred buildings is to memorialize Christ's victory over sin and death. Jesus died on the cross to take away the eternal consequences of sin, and he defeated death by not staying dead. On the cross, he suffered and sacrificed his human life in place of ours. He used the embarrassment of an instrument of capital punishment, a cross—in order to show us the horrid results of our rebelliousness against God, in order to show God's victory over the Evil One. Jesus carried a cross and then allowed himself to be nailed to it until all the life was poured out of him. He was then entombed several days to make the very real point that he was stone cold dead.

Here comes the miracle! Are you ready for this? After several days in the tomb, he was back, living again! It was the ultimate victory over that enemy called death. And just as God the Father performed the miracle of drying up the Jordan for the Israelites so that they could march victoriously into the Promised Land, Jesus the Son of God defeated death in order to give us victory over death. Now we can march victoriously into *our* Promised Land, and pass through death into eternal life in heaven with God. That is how much God loves you and me.

So we memorialize crosses in order to cement in our minds the fact that:

This is how much God loved the world: He gave his Son, his one and only Son. And this is why: so that no one need be destroyed;

*by believing in him, anyone can have a whole
and lasting life.*

John 3:16—*The Message*

As a bishop, I wear what is called a pectoral
cross over my vestments. It is sterling silver and
shows Jesus upon the cross wearing the crown
of a king and the vestments of a priest. It is called
a *Christus Victor,* because it presents Jesus as our
sacrifice, priest, and king all wrapped up in one
Savior, all the Jesus we will ever need for victo-
rious living! That silver cross was given to me in
the 1970s as a going away gift by my youth group
at that wonderful parish back in Texas. The youth
group did not realize they were actually giving
me a bishop's cross, and I was not about to tell
them and hurt their feelings. So I received the
cross gracefully and then put it away in my
jewelry box, figuring I would never wear it. It
sat there tarnishing for twenty years.

And then I was elected bishop! The first thing
I did was to get that cross out of the box and get
it shined up. The leaders of the parish placed it
over my head at my consecration. I had long
before discovered that God has a sense of humor,
but this was just plain miraculous fun!

Now when I put that cross over my head
every morning while dressing, I memorialize in

my heart and soul that great truth—God is present and active in my life; Jesus died for me and is giving me victory! And I am strengthened to proclaim by word and deed that Jesus Christ is Lord and Savior. The pectoral cross I wear is my "pile of rocks," the memorial I use to remind me of the miraculous victory God has wrought.

How about you? Do you have a "pile of rocks" memorializing your faith? Perhaps the church building of your youth? A religious article or medal piece you hold dear? A particular book God used to change your faith? Or maybe even a person alive or dead who guided you when you most needed it? These memorials can strengthen you and build up your faith. But for them to be real memorials giving you strength, you need to be aware of them and revisit them regularly.

Right now: pause from reading this book and think about your memorials. Bring them, one at a time, into your mind. Spend some time on each, recalling the circumstances that each memorial represents. As you examine each memorial, offer a prayer of thanks to our Lord for "helping you cross your Jordan" from exile and wandering to victory. Make this exercise imaginative and fun.

Chapter Six

Here Comes the
Bad Stuff!

Memorial Faith Has A Downside

In the last chapter, we examined the good points of Memorial Faith. It works! But Memorial Faith has a downside. And if we are not aware of the downside, we can get stuck in the Memorial Faith stage, and never progress down the road God has paved for us. Let's look at the shortcomings of Memorial Faith.

She had her memorial. She had been clutching it for years. It was a beautiful set of rosary beads her grandfather had given her as he lay dying. She was a young teenager who idolized her Grandpa. He had been her rock of stability in a continuous family earthquake. As he lay dying, Grandpa said to her, "Rachel, always keep these rosary beads. If you live a good life, we will see each other again when you die and join me in heaven."

She tried to live a good life. She really did. But she had some things going against her. Her parents were rather wrapped up in their careers, did not get along with each other, and tended to mistreat Rachel emotionally. Her parents were not religious in the least. They did not go to church, nor encourage her to go. With earthly pride, they said, "We don't want to prejudice her decision, so we're not going to teach her religion. When she grows up, she can decide for herself."

That was a fatal error on their part, because it meant Rachel would grow up with no spiritual grounding whatsoever, except for a kindly grandfather who had faith, but because of hostility from his son, could only share the faith with her by example and not by word.

Rachel was strong-willed, and tended to learn things the hard way: by making mistakes. Soon after her grandfather died, she went into a rebellion against her parents by drinking alcohol, taking drugs, and having sex. But she kept her rosary in her purse, and late at night if she was sober, she would hold those beads and think of her kind old grandfather. She would whisper, "Grandpa, I'm trying to be good so I can join you in heaven. But it's so hard, Grandpa. Mom and Dad don't seem to even care where I go or what I do. They just want to make money and buy stuff. I'm all alone without you. I don't know where to turn. Please help me, Grandpa." Then she would feel better, put the rosary beads back into her purse, and try to do things right for awhile. But, of course, Grandpa could not answer her prayer. And since she had no grounding in spirituality, she continued to swing from good behavior to destructive.

This continued through major drug events, several pregnancies, alienation and separation from her parents, and several suicide attempts. Through it all, she clutched her memorial, her rosary, and pleaded with her grandfather to save her. She would always get some sense of relief from holding her rosary, but it was never enough to keep her from doing the next wrong thing.

Eventually Rachel went into a rehab program and joined a Twelve Step group. That worked to get her sober, and she even began to get some things straightened out in her life. For the first time in years, she was able to hold a steady job. Her sponsor spent time with her, giving her wonderful guidance. But due to her lack of a spiritual grounding, she chose the rosary and the memory of her grandfather for her higher power. While psychologically this "higher power" gave Rachel a somewhat healthy focus outside herself, it was really not a higher power. It was just a string of olive wood beads, a memorial to a kind, dead man. And so she continued to struggle with wrong choices. Sexual encounters with various men were usually the most destructive.

She finally realized that these sexual encounters were her tortuous way of psychologically and even physically destroying herself, a way of turning the anger she had for her parents upon herself. She joined a Twelve Step group for sex addicts. And she was able, after some good

Twelve Step work, to improve her life regarding her sexuality.

It was not until she met a new Twelve Step sponsor who was a Christian that it all began to come together. Her sponsor invited her to church on Sunday, began talking with her about the "Living Higher Power," and eventually helped Rachel replace her bone-chilling loneliness with a loving relationship with Jesus Christ. One night, both the sponsor and Rachel got down on their knees, and Rachel made real amends to Almighty God, repented of her sins, and invited Jesus Christ to be her Lord and Savior.

In the days that followed, Rachel's life changed dramatically. She continued with her Twelve Step work, and eventually became a sponsor herself. But she also began her spiritual work in earnest, taking silent time each day to pray and read the Bible, getting involved in Bible studies and prayer groups, and taking on some ministries at the parish level. She was invited to join the church choir. That was where she really felt closest to God—she had always liked to sing, and singing in the choir gave her a chance to use her voice in ministry. Thus she grew as a Christian.

Rachel still carries her memorial in her purse, but it no longer contains a sense of magic for her.

It is still her memorial, but now that she has been grounded in a mature faith in Christ, she uses her memorial as it should be used—as a nice way to remember her grandfather. She has also learned how to use the rosary beads for prayer to God, rather than as an S.O.S. to a kindly, deceased grandfather.

The Mother of All Monuments

Now let's change the scene. Let's go back to my hometown: Schuylerville, New York. There's a great memorial to the Revolutionary War in Schuylerville: the Saratoga Battle Monument. It rises majestically over the Hudson Valley. When I was a kid, we used to be able to climb that monument, much like climbing the Washington Monument in Washington, D.C. But over the years the Monument deteriorated until it was unsafe to climb. Today, workers have just completed a restoration of the Monument, so that once again people can climb to the top and look out over the Battlefield and the Green Mountains of Vermont. I remember many such climbs and views when I was a boy. On the second story of the Saratoga Battle Monument are four niches, looking out in all four directions of the compass. Three of the niches are filled with busts of the heroic military leaders of that battle, the turning point of the American Revolution—Schuyler, Gates, and Morgan. But the fourth niche is vacant. No bust can be found there. It is the niche reserved for the real hero of the Battle of Saratoga—Benedict Arnold! Legend and record both state that in the heat of the battle and when the Americans were ready to bolt and run in the face of massive Red Coat opposition, Benedict rallied the troops by leading a charge against the British Army. Even though wounded in the leg, Arnold bravely and savagely led his troops forward, routing the British and turning the tide of battle to the Americans. Arnold was the real hero of Saratoga; but his niche is empty. Why? Why would this military hero not be given honor for his great leadership on the battlefield at Saratoga?

Treason! After the Battle of Saratoga, Benedict Arnold felt he had not been given the proper recognition he deserved. He became angry with his fellow Americans, and began to question the whole independence enterprise. Benedict Arnold became a traitor to the American cause, spying for the British. He was eventually found out, humiliated by the American public, and died in disgrace in England. All his acts of heroism and leadership as an American patriot were negated by his act of treason as a spy. Arnold's niche in the Saratoga Battle Monument will always be empty, and American history will always see him as the hero who turned traitor.

The Saratoga Battle Monument has for many years been a great memorial to our nation and the values we espouse. But what would have happened if we had never integrated those learnings into our lives and value system? Can you imagine your reaction if you found that we Schuylerites were focusing our full attention on that stone monument instead of on what it stood for . . . that we saw the monument as a magical protector of Schuylerville rather than as a symbol of America's quest for freedom . . . that we believed the monument had within itself some power to protect us from onslaughts and from becoming traitors . . . that we actually began to worship the stones or the three military heroes in its niches? The monument would at that point become a hindrance to societal progress rather than an instiller of responsibility.

Remembering that battle monument makes me realize what can happen to us when Memorial Faith dominates our lives—when allegiance to "The Church," whether a building or a concept, takes dominance over a relationship with the Head of the Church—or when the

"Bible" as a cold, sterile idol, takes dominance over a relationship with the Word-Made-Flesh—or when liturgy and ritual take on God-like properties and the God of our redemption somehow gets lost in the beautiful carvings of the baptismal font.

At several points in his earthly life, Jesus had to deal with just that kind of sin. Let me share with you one of those events. It was a hot day, even on top of the mountain. It was hot, and there was no breeze. It had been a long walk up. Jesus was over kneeling by a rock, praying. His three lieutenants were not far away, also kneeling in prayer. Peter thought, "I'll just nod off for a minute . . ." Well, let me quote the event from the Bible:

> Six days later, three of them saw that glory. Jesus took Peter and the brothers, James and John, and led them up a high mountain. His appearance changed from the inside out, right before their eyes. Sunlight poured from his face. His clothes were filled with light. Then they realized that Moses and Elijah were also there in deep conversation with him.

Peter broke in, "Master, this is a great moment! What would you think if I built three memorials here on the mountain—one for you, one for Moses, and one for Elijah?"

While he was going on like this, babbling, a light-radiant cloud enveloped them, and sounding from deep in the cloud a voice: "This is my Son, marked by my love, focus of my delight. Listen to him."

> *When the disciples heard it, they fell flat on their faces, scared to death. But Jesus came and touched them. "Don't be afraid." When they opened their eyes and looked around all they saw was Jesus, only Jesus.*
> Matthew 17:1-8—*The Message*

Part of me wishes that I could have been there that day to experience such a great event! Part of me wishes that today I might have just such a miraculous encounter with Jesus and friends. I would never doubt again, but would always have that vision to hold on to. What an introduction it would allow when I preached in a new setting: "Let me tell you about a mountaintop experience I had with Jesus . . ."

Of course, there is another part of me wishing that I might *never* have an experience like that. Most people would not believe me when I tried to explain what I saw! Some would think I was crazy! Even within myself, I'm not sure I want to get that close to Divinity while still on this earth. It would be too frightening!

But Peter, James, and John had no time to decide whether or not they wanted such a vision. There it was! One minute they were dozing in the still, hot air, and the next they were gazing on a mysteriously transfigured Jesus and two guys who had been dead for hundreds of years! How do you deal with that? If you are James or John, you stare, speechless! But if you are Peter the Extrovert, you jump right into the event, mouth first. Peter must have realized immediately that this was a miracle unfolding before his very eyes. By the conversation he witnessed before charging in, he somehow realized that one of Jesus' visitors was none other than Moses the Lawgiver—Moses, who had brought the people across the Red Sea, had delivered the Ten Commandments to the Israelites, and had led the people forty years in the wilderness, teaching them how to put those Commandments into everyday action. Of course there was a problem here for Peter: Moses had been dead for 1300 years! Peter suddenly remembered hearing about the Archangel Michael contending with the devil for Moses' carcass after he died (Jude 1:9). "So this event I'm living right here was the reason for the fight over Moses' body," Peter thought, "I'm not cracking up. And this is not a dream. So the only conclusion I can draw is that I am in the middle of a miraculous vision right now!" Peter somehow realized that this was a great miracle event, and that the conversation he was hearing between Jesus and Moses centered on how Jesus would accomplish by his cross in Jerusalem what Moses had not been able to fully accomplish in the wilderness by teaching the Law.

Peter then recognized the other visitor—the great prophet Elijah! Dead 800 years! Last seen heading for heaven in a chariot of fire! "Well, he's baaack!" thought Peter. And then he realized listening to the further conversation between Jesus and Elijah that the fulfillment of all the prophesies the prophets had spun about a Messiah who would come to liberate the people of Israel were now being achieved in Jesus.

All this Peter observed, almost in a heartbeat. And he was bursting with excitement! He simply could not contain himself. He had to insert himself into this monumental conversation. And in so doing, he pulled the old Aunt Gertrude act. "OK," Peter yelled, "Let's take a snapshot of this for my scrapbook. Jesus, you get between Moses and Elijah. Elijah, did you bring your chariot? Maybe we can get that in there. And how about the two stone tablets, Moses?"

Well, maybe it did not happen just like that.

But it would have if they had cameras back then. Peter did the first century equivalent. He wanted to build a monument—tabernacles or shelters to memorialize the event. Peter wanted very much to memorialize the event so that others could come to the mountain, gaze upon the booths, and realize that Jesus really was the fulfillment of all the Law and the Prophets. He had good intentions. "Lord, it is good that we (translate 'I') are here. Let me build three Memorials, one for you and one for Moses and one for Elijah."

Can't you just see the three look over at Peter? Moses may have mumbled, "This guy sounds like my loudmouth brother Aaron—all words and no sense!" Elijah may have seen a piece of his replacement Elisha in Peter—"Lord, your head assistant there is just like Elisha was—he doesn't get it, does he?" And Jesus probably said, "He's my Rock. He just doesn't know it yet. What can I say?"

So at that point the Heavenly Father decided to make it really clear to Peter. God the Creator arrived on the scene, as He often did in the Bible, in the midst of a cloud. Get ready, Peter: here comes the Theophany! Here's an unholy translation of what the Father said to Peter: "Peter, stop interrupting! This is my Son. Just shut up and listen!"

It is interesting that even though Peter really experienced that Theophany and wanted to memorialize it, he still had the capacity to sin. Shortly thereafter, he denied Jesus three times in order to save his own life. He still had a crisis of faith.

Do you think that perhaps Peter was one who tended toward Memorial Faith rather than Miracle Faith? Maybe that is why Jesus wanted nothing to do with building a memorial to the Transfiguration, and even forbade Peter to talk about it. You see, the faith lesson here is Peter wanted to enshrine in *stone* the Law, the Prophets, and the Gospel, while Jesus wanted to enshrine in our *hearts* the Law, the Prophets, and the Gospel. Jesus knew that Peter's approach would harden the Law, the Prophets, and the Gospel into cold, legalistic, religious oppression, while Jesus' approach would melt the Law, the Prophets, and the Gospel into warm, luscious Grace.

You know, I have to laugh when I realize that Peter's story is often *my* story . . . and perhaps yours, too! Let me explain.

I've been struggling with just that conflict for a long, long time—trying to memorialize faith traditions, and thus suck the life right out of them. It is a part of every person's faith journey, even yours. I call it a *faith drift*, a drifting backward from our faith development. I may experience Miracle Faith, a great gift. But if I don't sustain a relationship with the Miracle Maker, there is a natural drift in my life toward a cold, hard Memorial Faith.

As I was thinking about this, I said to myself, "My gosh! This happens in the Church as we move from generation to generation in a congregation!" It's kind of like the story of three generations!

The First Generation

First Generation Faith is characterized by the word "conversion." This generation has shared a miraculous vision—a deep, penetrating realization that God is present and active. In our First Generation Faith, we build a spiritual monument to our conversion by ritualizing it. We want the process of that conversion to happen to others exactly the way that it happened to us!

So we memorialize our experience, sometimes encasing it in a spiritual tabernacle to make sure it is not reinterpreted in any way. To protect the authenticity of our conversion, we build a legalistic compound around it regarding just how others can share and live out that experience.

Without realizing it, we are focusing on the conversion event by memorializing it, rather than focusing on the God who converted us in order to have a relationship of intimacy with us.

So we share our ritual experience with the Second Generation and try to get the Second Generation to have the same experience or at least to keep alive the memorial of our experience. We are puzzled when they don't have the same zeal. Not sure how to proceed, we go into denial regarding our children's lack of faith, and assume it will come with time. But the key deficiency is that we ourselves have somehow failed to maintain our own "first love" with God, and thus have only Memorial Faith to pass on to the Second Generation.

Let's look at this drift through the story of Joshua and the Israelites. Joshua's generation— let's call them the First Generation—were the first to enter the Land of Milk and Honey. And they did it with flair! The twelve-stone monument they built after the miraculous crossing of the Jordan was the vehicle the First Generation used to replay their river crossing experience to the Second Generation. It appears that they tended to memorialize the crossing of the Jordan with more fervor than they memorialized the God who enabled the crossing. Their hope was that the Second Generation would so venerate the First Generation's miraculous crossing of the Jordan that they would have the same fervor of faith their parents had.

The Second Generation

Let's assume the role of the Second Generation for a moment. For us, faith takes a different approach altogether. While we have heard from the previous one about a miraculous conversion experience, and while we respect the First Generation's great fervor, it is difficult for us to make it our own experience. Try as we might by living it through our parents' eyes, we just can't see what all the excitement is about. The First Generation talks and talks about the monument—but we can't seem to understand what they are really telling us. We see our parents' "monument" and respect it, but we don't have the fundamental conversion experience itself. Since we have not experienced it ourselves, we stay with the faith community simply out of respect for our elders. We have a strong commitment to the monument while not fully understanding the reason for the monument. We tell our own children about the monument but can't recall the underlying principle for the building of the monument. We have sunk deeply into maintaining a Memorial Faith, seeing ritual and ceremony as the spiritual goal, rather than a personal relationship with the Living God.

In Joshua's world, the next generation after the Jordan River crossing enjoyed living in the Promised Land to which they had been brought, and tried to stay true to the traditions Joshua and the First Generation had taught them. But aside from returning to the twelve-stone monument down there by the Jordan once in awhile, and taking a half-hearted stab at living by the Laws the First Generation had taught them, there was little substance to their faith in the Living God. They continued to join the army as their parents had, and continued to drive out the Canaanites, but they did not quite have the right focus. They did not remember that the reason they were driving the Canaanites out was to protect the Israelites from picking up their polytheistic customs. They thought they were driving the Canaanites out so they could acquire their land! And so when this new generation of Israelites experienced a pocket of particularly resistant Canaanites, they just left them there, in time beginning to trade with them. You might ask, "Why were they so stupid? Why couldn't they just obey God and rid the land of the

Canaanites?" The answer is that the Israelites were human, like you and me. While they had the intention of clearing the land of Canaanites, little problems cropped up. One group was especially hard to clear out, and so, the Israelite leaders reasoned that it was not worth the effort to clear them out: "It's such a small group, we will just leave them be, and let them die out." Another group of Canaanites may have proved to be friendly and probably volunteered to teach the Israelites how to farm the land: "Well, we will let them stay on the land because they can help us." Little by little, the Second Generation of Israelites, by living for short-term gains rather than long-term gains, disobeyed God big time!

We do the same thing today. Someone totally dedicated to good health and nourishing food motivates us to reform our ways. In secular terms, they are "First Generation Faith," and we are "Second." So having been motivated to try for good health and dietary practices by the totally dedicated "First Generation" health nut, we decide to try. Then little problems begin to present themselves, making it difficult to maintain our regimen: "I sprained my ankle; I'd better not work out while it is healing." And you know what doesn't happen after the sprain heals! Or someone waylays our diet: "Oh, come on," they say. "You can at least eat one. One won't hurt you. It may be fattening, but you can make it up tomorrow." So we eat it! And you know what happens tomorrow, don't you? Second Generation Faith is like that.

So the Second Generation of Israelites fell into Memorial Faith. They followed the rituals of the First Generation, but played fast and loose with the Miracle Maker and the life He called them to. They had the form of faith but not the substance.

The Third Generation

Now let's be the Third Generation. When left to our own devices we often drift into what might be called Misplaced Faith. Due to our mobile society of displaced generations, and because grandparents often hesitate to share faith with their grandchildren lest they offend their children, we Third Generation people often hear little if anything about the miraculous conversion experience of our grandparents. We see the Second Generation's commitment to the monument, but can't understand why they are so committed to a boring monument! In time we give up on the monument, and may find a conversion experience of our own, often misplaced, and start the whole process over again in a new venue.

For a good illustration of this whole business, let's look at America in the nineteenth century. The First Generation experienced the Great Awakening and became a great evangelical generation (Miracle Faith). The Second Generation saw but did not experience the Great Awakening, so they experienced only the liturgical trappings and language of the revival (Memorial Faith). The Third Generation knew nothing of the Great Awakening their grandparents had gone through; the Second Generation was too busy maintaining hardened rituals to remember what the rituals really symbolized or the God for whom the rituals were intended. So the Third Generation had neither Miracle Faith nor Memorial Faith. They distrusted the rituals, because the rituals had no power for them. So they found their own Miracle Faith. In some cases this new Miracle Faith propelled them back to Jesus. In the Episcopal Church and later in the Methodist Church, the Third Generation discovered the High Church Movement and the Broad Church Movement. But many of the Third Generation joined cultic or heretical groups, and these movements gave them the same sense of the fervor experienced by their grandparents. They became

Unitarians, Mormons, Christian Scientists, etc. Many just drifted away from church altogether. Their primary allegiance became the Grange, the Masonic Temple, and the political party. Not knowing Christian Miracle Faith or Christian Memorial Faith, they often adopted unchristian Misplaced Faith.

Back to Joshua and company: the Third Generation simply did not go on spiritual pilgrimage to the twelve-stone monument down by the Jordan. For all we know, the monument may have even washed away in a flood! It is never mentioned again in the Bible. So the Third Generation became syncretistic—a mistaken combination of two different and conflicting belief systems. Because pockets of Canaanites were allowed by the Second Generation to stay on the land and in fact to interact with the Israelites, the Third Generation saw the lifestyle of the Canaanites as normative. The Third Generation picked up the attractive aspects of Canaanite worship, and integrated it into their own lives. They unwittingly allowed the hard work of their enthusiastic grandparents and the grudging work of their acquiescing parents to go for naught. The Third Generation, having neither the Miracle Faith of the First Generation, nor the Memorial Faith of the Second Generation, adopted a Misplaced Faith, and started the whole process over with a syncretistic religion. They couldn't see any reason to follow very difficult laws when all the other people around them were living it up. The Book of Judges puts it rather succinctly:

> *And the people of Israel did what was evil in the sight of the Lord and served the Ba'als; and they forsook the Lord, the God of their fathers, who had brought them out of the land of Egypt; they went after other gods of the peoples who were round about them, and bowed down to them; and they provoked the Lord to anger.*
>
> Judges 2:11-13

Generational Drift—
The American Version of False Gods

We have seen this phenomenon as recently as the twentieth century. Throughout the late 1940s, '50s, and even into the '60s, a great revival in church membership swept America. Churches were bursting at the seams, and new church buildings were going up seemingly on every corner. Attendance records were broken every year.

During the Second World War, the G.I. Generation had stared evil in the eye in Europe and in the Pacific. They had seen the power of God working through the allied governments and armed forces. With victory came a great sense of thanksgiving to God—Christian faith was renewed in America. So the G.I. Generation returned to church in big numbers, and they brought their "post-war baby boom" kids, bringing about burgeoning Sunday schools.

But something was missing: a personal faith witness! The First Generation saw God at work, but did not know quite how to relate to Him. So they went "ritualistic," finding fulfillment in church attendance and in the great liturgies and music of the Church. Instead of passing on a powerful Miracle Faith, the faith that had defeated Hitler, they passed on a smug Memorial Faith, ritualistic and hollow. Their faith development drifted backward. Without maintaining a personal witness to the power of God and without a continuing relationship with the Miracle Maker, this is what they unknowingly passed on to their kids.

The "post-war baby boom" kids—let's call them the Second Generation—dutifully went to Sunday school and church, but were not sure *why* they were going. They received a lot of instruction in treating others with respect and in developing good self-esteem, but they did not hear much about the God of the Bible, His great power over evil, or His desire to have a personal relationship with people through Jesus Christ. And they did not hear much about repentance and coming under the power of the Holy Spirit. So they trudged along through church and Sunday school, learning proper rituals and social ministries, and slowly moving into positions of church leadership. Because the Second World War was simply a history lesson to them, they did not have in their hearts a sense of the struggle between good and evil so clearly experienced by their parents. Life became relativistic for the Second Generation, as theology, ethics, and morality all moved toward intellectual relativism.

Eventually the Second Generation began leading the Church, and "relativism," "inclusion," and "diversity" moved to center stage. Personal commitment to Christ and a definitive Judeo-Christian Ethic were moved stage right and out of the mainstream. The Second Generation began to see traditional church leadership and values as rather restrictive on their expansive lifestyle. They cast around for an objective for their faith, a new value system.

And they found it in social issues—racial inequities, the Cold War and the question of nuclear armament, gender issues, the environment, the evils of nationalism, and sexual orientation and behavior. This is the faith perspective they gave their kids—the Third Generation.

The Third Generation was confused about the whole question of God. If, as their parents had said, "it does not matter what you have faith *in* as long as you are sincere," then why not pick a faith that is new and easy? They became interested in a whole plethora of faith-choices—cults, witchcraft, Satanism, astrology, psychics, parapsychology, new age religions, East Asian religions, and even their parents' idolization of materialism. They saw no reason to go to those traditional churches their grandparents and parents fostered—*boring*! The post-modern era moved squarely into society, and was not pleased with the options offered by the traditional churches.

While we are beginning to see that many of the Third Generation *are* coming back to the Christian tradition, albeit with their own post-modern slant, we see a number of them casting about for a new ethic, a new morality, a new god. It is still too soon to tell where this is all going.

What I have been getting at is that Memorial Faith has some real limitations when there is no Miracle Faith involved. Something happens to Memorial Faith when it is not plugged into the Power Source. It is like an old lamp that stops being used. When it is no longer plugged in, it loses it effectiveness. It becomes old and dusty, and eventually gets sentenced to the attic.

And so it goes for us—generation after generation:

1. We find a wonderful intimacy with God, and build a monument of elaborate liturgy and ritual in order to praise Him publicly. But in concentrating on teaching our kids the liturgy for praising God, we often spend too little time teaching them intimacy with God. In so doing, we unwittingly get our kids hooked on the monument rather than on God.

2. Consequently our children don't get to know God that well. They get somewhat committed to the "Liturgy Monument," but without intimacy with God, the monument does not go the distance for them. They, of course, do not teach their kids intimacy with God, because they themselves have no idea what that is. And though they do know the liturgy, they do not have the time or the inclination to commit their kids to the "Liturgy Monument."

3. One generation later, our grandchildren receive nothing but mixed signals from grandparents and parents. They can't figure out what the big deal is about going to church, and so they cast about for something new.

A Bishop's Perspective

As a bishop I see lots of parishes. I'm in a different church building every week, meeting lots of great people, preaching to them, teaching them, and trying to encourage them to be faith sharers. I've seen the First-Second-Third Generation Syndrome more times than I can count. Sometimes it is me! I have to be careful that in all this pomp and circumstance of special vestments and my shepherd's staff that I don't lose the Dave Bena God called me to be. It is so easy to fall into the First-Second-Third Generation trap! It is the natural way of churches and organizations, as well as individuals. Look at a lot of the stalwart organizations that used to be so influential in America, many of which grew up in the World War I and II worlds— veteran groups, fraternal orders, professional/ agricultural organizations. We are seeing these organizations either gone or mere shadows of their former selves because they have suffered the First-Second-Third Generation Syndrome. I can't do anything about these great organizations, but I do have some responsibility for the Church. How do we stem the tide of lost members in the Church? Miracle Faith!

Professor Howard Hanchey has done seminal work in the area of Parish Drift in his important book, *Church Growth and the Power of Evangelism* (1990, Cowley Publications). Hanchey claims that there are two types of churches—the survival-oriented Church and the mission-oriented Church. I am now going to loosely follow his descriptions of these Churches in order to show Memorial Faith and Miracle Faith from a parish perspective.

Churches with a Maintenance Mentality

Churches with a survival mentality simply want to do that—maintain what they've got, and survive. They tend to protect the "monument." They do not want to change anything lest they somehow lose what they've got. They have turned inward and decided that their purposes are twofold: to care for their membership and to maintain their important traditions—in two words, Memorial Faith. Not particularly interested in converting anyone or gaining new members, they put little emphasis on evangelism. They are willing to accept new members who don't try to change anything, especially the liturgy. Their money is mostly spent on themselves, and they justify putting no money into outreach by saying that they pay the pastor to do outreach. They are not too interested in Christian Education except for the Sunday school "so that our kids will understand our heritage." A personal experience with Jesus Christ is seldom talked about, and is even sometimes looked on with suspicion as some "right-wing fanaticism."

The perplexing thing about the survival-minded Church is that by taking this approach, that church dies rather than survives! Christianity was never meant to be a closed club or an inwardly directed group. This approach is characteristic of Memorial Faith. Although times and priorities have changed from the Fabulous Fifties when people were pouring into these houses of worship, many churches are still doing business the way they did when there was little need to woo new congregants—and so they are ministering to fewer and fewer congregants. Today's population drives by these great worship edifices on their way to their kids' Sunday morning soccer tournaments, having little interest in what is going on "in there." They are not going to darken the door of a church without a personal invitation. And they will probably not get an invitation because many of the members think that "religion is personal" and that "to invite someone to church is to commit the crime of proselytizing." Since so few church members claim a life-giving relationship with the person of Jesus, this church will not pass on the beauty of Jesus to the next generation, and it will not seek to bring others to this relationship. It has become a maintenance-minded Church, maintaining old traditions that no longer touch lives. The result is inevitable—death. And to the extent that you and I try to retain the status quo of Memorial Faith, we are part of this inevitable death!

Churches With a Mission Mentality

Hanchey goes on to describe the mission-mentality Church. This church can represent Miracle Faith. The members of this church are outward looking, seeking to transmit the Gospel by word and deed—sending out missionaries to spiritually feed the souls of lost humankind, and to physically feed the bodies of hungry people. They are alive with the Love of God! They consider a personal relationship with a loving, life-changing God central to being the Church. They believe the Bible when it says that the Church is the Body of Christ, with Christ as the Head. The members, called disciples, really see themselves as part of the loving, healing Body of Christ, and are not embarrassed to ask the Holy Spirit to keep transforming every area of their lives, to equip them just as He equipped those first disciples of Jesus.

So the healthy mission-minded Church is interested in the mission of the Gospel— to "restore all people to unity with God and each other in Christ" (The Book of Common Prayer, 1979, Catechism, page 855). The members continually invite family and friends to their church. They conduct *exciting* Bible-centered education programs for all ages, following the age-old dictum, "It is a sin to *bore* people with the Gospel." They are concerned that their children have a chance to hear the Gospel in their own context, and are willing to spend as much money and time on their children's spiritual development as they do on their academic and social development!

And they know that Miracle Faith can be perverted into an antiseptic, evangelical system of gaining members unless it is sustained by daily prayer, scripture reading, and faithful reception of Holy Communion. So the mission-minded Church seeks communal worship that is filled with excitement and spiritual strength. They are willing to take a chance on something new in worship if it might issue forth in more disciples growing closer to Jesus. And they are generous givers of their financial resources, taking the tithe (giving a tenth of income) seriously. This generosity of spirit rubs off on their children, who instead of peeling off church when they get to college, look for ways they can stay connected. These people expect miracles, and they see them!

Where Are You—Mission or Maintenance?

So where are you in your faith journey—survival-minded or mission-minded? Memorial Faith or Miracle Faith? On one side or the other? Or somewhere in the middle with attributes from both mentalities? God loves us so much that He craves intimacy with us. This forgiving and loving God has shown us in His Son Jesus that His wish is to embrace us through eternity! It is time for us to break out of the cocoon of Memorial Faith and fly freely into the power of Miracle Faith.

I must admit I have had my supply of

Memorial Faith moments, months, and seeming millennia! When I joined the Episcopal Church we used the 1928 Book of Common Prayer. Having been raised in a liturgical church, I liked a set liturgy. And I liked the 1928 Prayer Book. It was old, stuffy, and churchy. I liked that— it had "church language" that I would not use in my office or down on the flight line. I could compartmentalize church by using two languages, one for the world and one for worship. I also thought the 1928 Book was very eloquent and had a great way of phrasing theological language.

Therefore, I was not thrilled when we went into Prayer Book revision! And did we ever go through Prayer Book revision! It went on for years! There were the Prayer Book Supplements, the 1967 Holy Communion Booklet, the "Zebra Book," the "Green Book." I saw the revision process as not a revision at all, but a rewrite! I thought the proposed language was too pedestrian, the theology too wishy-washy, and the awesomeness of God being frittered away. In 1979, the new Prayer Book was approved, and became the normative book in the Episcopal Church.

Eventually the 1979 Book of Common Prayer became a new friend, but first I had to get in touch with why I was really so angry about changing prayer books. What I finally realized was that I had made the 1928 Prayer Book a monument to my faith. I had come into the Episcopal Church with that book! How dare someone change it on me? Memorial Faith—I had it in spades! It took a shaking up of my faith, until I realized that I was supposed to worship the God of the 1928 Prayer Book and the 1979 Prayer Book, not the books themselves. I had to surrender that 1928 Book, and let God, not a prayer book, be God in my life.

In that moment of realization, I stepped back into the stream of mission-minded faith. I had to move again from Memorial Faith to Miracle Faith. Jesus Christ died for me, a sinner, and then he was raised that I might in turn be raised to eternal life—a miracle! That miracle is so much more important than the wording of a Prayer Book. Live into the miracle, not with the fear that your Memorial Faith will be threatened!

Alas for me, now I hear that we may be in the first stages of yet another Book of Common Prayer. Will I go through this process again? Probably. For people to grow in their faith, life seems to be constantly moving from Memorial Faith to Miracle Faith to Memorial Faith to Miracle Faith. But without an understanding of this ebb and flow movement, we can get stuck in the stultifying stage of Memorial Faith.

Unless our faith is shaken up sometimes and renewed, we will continually slip into the subtle temptation of comfortable Memorial Faith. We will do that as persons, and we will do that as parishes. We need the Holy Spirit to come in and shake us up, and then empower us with His Life to take hold of Miracle Faith. To do that we need to continually confess our lesser gods, and let God's Spirit give us the power we need.

So it goes with our faith commitment. God has a wonderful plan for us. This includes salvation for us both here and in heaven. It includes living lives of character. And above all, it includes becoming carriers of God's "no strings love."

But often we forget the real priority of a relationship with God, and instead settle for the lower priority—comfortable living on earth! So we use Christianity for our own self-fulfillment, or business success, or a posh retirement, or successful kids we can brag about, or the right home and material possessions. We build a monument of earthly success and forget God's priority of a faith-filled, character-filled relationship with Jesus Christ. We need to move from Memorial Faith to Miracle Faith.

The Good, Bad, and Ugly of Memory Faith

Chapter Seven

Memories That Keep Us Cookin'

Now Let's Switch Gears

I've spent a lot of pages talking about the positives and negatives of Memorial Faith, and how we can move from the deadening waters of Memorial Faith into the beautiful seas of Miracle Faith. Now let's go back and look at that other stage of faith—Memory Faith. I'll do the same thing with Memory Faith that I did with Memorial Faith—a chapter on the good points of Memory Faith, then a chapter on its negative points. And then I'll show you how we can move from the Memory Faith trap into the freedom of Miracle Faith. So let's explore the positives of Memory faith.

Memories are important. In organizational life, there is something called "institutional memory." An organization's institutional memory is carried from year to year by two instruments—archival material (computer data, newsletters, correspondence, memos, etc.), and peoples' memories. Archival material gets put in the archives and is seldom looked at again. So it is really people who carry the institutional memory of an organization. In a small headquarters, for instance, it is dangerous to change a whole staff at once because you chance losing the institutional memory or history of the organization, and then as the wise statement of old states, "They who ignore their history are doomed to repeat it!"

This can happen in a church headquarters, or even in a parish church. In our own diocesan office, we experienced a rapid turnover in personnel when one diocesan bishop retired and another was elected to take his place. We wound up with very little institutional memory to keep us from repeating the mistakes of the past. So we often talked with those who used to occupy our chairs, to get a historical view of the office and its policies, to learn why they did what they did, and to understand the interpersonal relationships of those people who sat at our desks before we arrived. Until we could understand all this, we could not successfully move into new ministry and cast off in the new direction we sensed God was leading us. Memories are important in building initiative and maintaining momentum!

In the local parish, the new rector usually arrives after the old one leaves. Unless the staff and/or lay leaders can spend considerable time acquainting the new rector with "programs and people," ministries and people will very likely get lost in the shuffle. Very often, those who get lost are the elderly and shut-ins. More thought needs to be put into the process of changing pastors in a local church. Memory is important here.

Memories are also important in families. As I write this, my mother is 95 years old. My father died many years ago; my grandparents have also been deceased a long time; and my mother's siblings are dying off. My brothers and sisters and I have begun to realize that when Mother dies, our family history may very well die as well. Not much has been written down. We have only some anecdotal material. So some time ago, we began asking Mother to let her memory take us all back in time to her childhood and early adult years, and to tell us all she remembered about her family history. It has been fascinating to hear her memories of parents and grandparents, of life in the early twentieth century, and of her memories of my father as a boy (they knew each other as children), of their courtship and early years of marriage in the Great Depression. Listening to her has helped us all understand more about our heritage, our faith, and ourselves.

Memories are important to world religions. We Christians believe that God inspired people to write Holy Scriptures. Before the age of written history, our faith community sat around the fire at night reciting its memories, and repeating those memories faithfully to their children until they were sure the children had the stories down pat. Then that young generation, when grown, carried on the same program with *their* children. And so the Holy Spirit was able, through the memories of the faith community, to get the faith stories transmitted through the generations, adding to them, until it was time for these stories to be written down. Then, in addition to the oral tradition, written histories were made of the people of God. And so today we know about the crossing of the Jordan River by Joshua and company; we know about the life, crucifixion, and resurrection of Jesus; we know about all the other memories of our spiritual ancestors. Without these memories, now committed to writing, we would not know who we are as the people of God.

Memory Faith—A Biblical Perspective

Where can I find an example of how important Memory Faith is to us? As I think about the Holy Scriptures, my mind runs to two parallel events that were directed by God and were meant to be remembered regularly by the People of God, one in the Old Testament and one in the New.

An Old Testament Example

Let's look at the Old Testament event first—the Passover, faithfully celebrated by Jews every year for thousands of years.

> *Then Moses called all the elders of Israel, and said to them, "Select lambs for yourselves according to your families, and kill the Passover lamb. Take a bunch of hyssop and dip it in the blood which is in the basin, and touch the lintel and the two doorposts with the blood which is in the basin . . ." Then the people of Israel went and did so; as the Lord had commanded Moses and Aaron, so they did.*
>
> *At midnight the Lord smote all the first-born in the land of Egypt, from the first-born of Pharaoh who sat on his throne to the first-born of the captive who was in the dungeon, and all the first born of the cattle.*
>
> Exodus 12:21-22, 24, 28-29

What a memory! That is a story you do not forget. As we know from Bible history, the Hebrews had been a nomadic people wandering around the lands we now call Israel. At one point in their history, one of the Hebrews, Joseph, was betrayed by his brothers and sold into slavery in

Egypt. As the years went by, Joseph distinguished himself in the presence of the Egyptian pharaoh, and was elevated to a position roughly equivalent to that of Prime Minister. When a famine came to that part of the world, Joseph was instrumental in saving the people of Egypt. In one of God's most interesting turnabouts of all time, the people of Israel, instead of starving, found themselves safe in Egypt, as Joseph forgave his brothers and brought the people of Israel down to live there with him. And they stayed in Egypt several hundred years. They grew in number and they prospered.

Years later, long after Joseph had died, a new pharaoh came to power. He distrusted this large body of non-Egyptians living in his land, and decided to enslave these Hebrews.

Moses was a Hebrew who should have been murdered at birth, but through another interesting turn of Godly events, was brought up in the royal household of Pharaoh as an adopted son! Moses received a first class education, the type of education he would later need to become the leader of the Israelites. And then, because of a murder Moses committed, he had to flee Egypt and live a number of years in exile. In the fullness of God's time, God brought him back to Egypt and used his leadership to convince

Pharaoh to set the Hebrews free. Through a number of plagues—blood in the water, frogs, gnats, flies, death of cattle, boils, hail, locusts, darkness, and finally the death of the first born—Pharaoh was convinced to set them free.

Returning now to the memory of the Passover, we see that the ritual killing of lambs and the sprinkling of the lambs' blood on doorposts served as a benchmark event, the memory of which has motivated people and nations ever since to place their whole trust in God, the great deliverer. On that occasion so many years ago, the Hebrews obediently trusted God and did what Moses told them to do. They killed the "Passover Lambs," and then sprinkled the blood of the lambs on their doorposts. And so it was that when the Angel of Death came through Egypt taking the first born as God's retribution for Pharaoh's stubbornness, he "passed over" the homes with blood on their doorposts. When Pharaoh saw what had happened, he realized for a moment that he was up against more than just a Hebrew slave population; he was up against their very powerful God! He called Moses and pleaded with him to get the Hebrews out of Egypt immediately, before more calamities struck Egypt. Moses complied, and the next morning they were on the move toward the Promised Land!

Of course, Pharaoh then had a little time to figure out that the freeing of these slaves was costing him big bucks. In his fear of losing the wealth the Hebrews had produced for him, he forgot all about the recent death plague, and set out with his army to bring back the Hebrew slaves. The victory by the Hebrews who crossed over the sea on foot, and the defeat of Pharaoh, who drowned trying to cross the Sea, ended that chapter of the history of the Jewish people.

But the memory was not forgotten! The memory has been told and retold in Sabbath school and Sunday school for ages since. Memory Faith!

There's the story of little Johnny who came home from Sunday school and his mother asked him what he had learned that day. "Well, Mom," Johnny said, "It was like this. Pharaoh's army was chasing Moses' army, and Moses was in full retreat. Suddenly they were backed up against the Red Sea. So Moses called in artillery, naval gunfire from ships, and air strikes from aircraft carriers, and they pulverized Pharaoh's army for awhile. Meanwhile Moses got the engineers to build great pontoon bridges, and Moses and his army crossed over the sea on the pontoon bridges. When they got across, and just when Pharaoh and his army were half way across the bridge, Moses called in more air strikes which destroyed the pontoon bridges, leaving Pharaoh and his army to drown." When he had finished his tale, his mother replied, "Now Johnny, are you sure your teacher told you it happened *that* way?" "Well, Mom," Johnny shot back, "if I told you what she really said happened, you'd never believe it!"

The whole Passover Story is unbelievable unless you have Memory Faith. The Covenant God made with the people of Israel was in the blood of the Passover lamb. By being obedient to God's Covenant, the people were saved by the blood they had sprinkled on their doorposts. They were literally saved from death by the blood of the Passover lamb! This memory tells us about our God and His deep love for us. No matter how mucked-up we get, either by our own design or by the craftiness of our enemies, God is there for us, seeing us through, giving us power to "pass over" into freedom.

A New Testament Example

Which leads me to the second scripture memory, which relates directly to the one I have just described—the Passover meal Jesus shared with his disciples just before he was crucified.

> *When it was time, he sat down, all the apostles with him, and said, "You've no idea how much I have looked forward to eating this Passover meal with you before I enter my time of suffering. It's the last one I'll eat until we all eat it together in the kingdom of God . . ."*

Taking bread, he blessed it, broke it, and gave it to them, saying, "This is my body, given for you. Eat it in my memory."

> *He did the same with the cup after supper, saying, "This cup is the new covenant written in my blood, blood poured out for you . . ."*
> Luke 22:14-20—*The Message*

Here we have Jesus and his disciples celebrating the annual memory of the Passover, which Jews have faithfully celebrated every year up to the present day. But at this particular Passover meal, which Christians call the Last Supper because it was probably the last meal Jesus shared with his disciples before he was crucified, Jesus departed from the traditional Passover meal script. In the original script, the emphasis is on reliving the Passover event of Moses and the company of the Hebrews. Jesus changed the script and gave it a new meaning. When Jesus said to his disciples, "This bread is my body given for you . . . this cup is my blood shed for you for the forgiveness of sins," he was *declaring himself to be the Passover Lamb!* His disciples must have just about fallen over when he said that. No one was supposed to change the Passover script, much less insert himself into it! Jesus did just that. You'll remember that when I wrote of the original Passover event, I said that the blood of the Passover Lamb was what saved the people. The shed blood of the lamb kept the Israelites from experiencing death, and set the stage for their flight to freedom. Well, when Jesus on the occasion of his Last Supper declared himself to be the Passover Lamb, he was setting the stage for the same thing to happen on a universal level. The next day, he actually would become the sacrificial Passover Lamb who would set his people free from sin, and this act of sacrifice would take place on the hard wood of a cross. Unbeknownst to themselves, the people of Israel and the whole universe were enslaved not by some Egyptian Pharaoh, but by their addiction to sin (and you and I are part of this universe and have the same addictive tendencies). The sin of humankind had put every human into bondage.

This act of rebelliousness on the part of humankind was a lot like any addiction today. The addictive behavior feels good at first and seems to provide a way to freedom from the problems we are encountering. But eventually the addiction takes over our lives and enslaves us. Even though we may crave freedom from the addiction, we soon begin to believe that we cannot live without the addiction. The only way to freedom from the addiction is to admit we are enslaved, give up our enslaved life to a new and more powerful force (God), and begin cooperating with God so He can work change in us. In trying to win freedom from our slavery to sin, we likewise have to admit that we are enslaved by it, give up our enslaved life to a new and more powerful force (the sacrificial death of Jesus on the cross), and begin cooperating with God to work change in us.

At the Last Supper, Jesus was beginning a great "tell and show" for his disciples who would travel down through the ages to you and me. At the Last Supper he would "tell" his disciples that he was the Passover Lamb whose blood would set them free from sin and would guarantee the forgiveness of their rebellious sins. And the next day on the cross, he would "show" it by allowing his body to be broken and his blood to be shed. His blood would indeed set us free from bondage.

Jesus' Passover meal provides a follow-on memory to the Passover event of Moses. Just as Jews have relived the Passover Event for thousands of years and found strength and solace in the memory, so Christians have for the last two thousand years relived the Last Supper regularly. Sharing that Meal kindles the memory of what Jesus has done for us. It gives us strength to live the Christian life. In a strange way we cannot explain, every time we relive the Meal, we somehow receive Jesus into our lives in a unique way—the bread and the wine become the Real Presence of Jesus.

Many Christians call this memory a Sacrament (some call it an Ordinance), an outward and visible sign of an inward and spiritual grace instituted by Christ. God uses this memorial act to change us . . . and also to move us into Miracle Faith, thus strengthening us for His service. And so our Memory Faith provides the touchstone by which we continually experience the grace of God in Jesus Christ. We are reminded of the freedom Jesus has won for us, and this memory keeps us from falling back into slavery.

Letting the Holy Spirit Out of the Bible and Into Our Lives!

Which brings us to our own personal faith journeys. I see the story of the Israelites being freed from slavery in Egypt as somehow *my* story; the story of Jesus and the Last Supper as also *my* story . . . as *our* story, yours and mine. Why else would the Holy Spirit go to such pains to get these memories recorded? These memories are recorded so that we might be saved from slavery to sin, meaninglessness, and futility—from hell! How do we unlock our minds, our sterile view of Bible times, and let God flow into us—opening us up to see new beauty? How can I let the Bible turn my *blahs* into "Ahas?"

I see these Bible memories reminding me that God loves me deeply and is there for me both while I am on earth as well as when my eyes close on this earth and open to behold the beautiful gaze of Jesus. My faith journey is a bit like that of the Israelites in Egypt—confused, enslaved, hopeless. But just as God made a way for the Israelites through the blood of the Passover Lamb, God has made a way for me through the blood of Jesus, the Passover Lamb. In so doing, He has enabled me in my journey to pass over from slavery to freedom; from the futility of knowing I will die here on this earth some day to the hope of knowing that God is preparing a wonderful home for me. The memories God has created in the Bible offer us the roadmap to new meaning and hope! Memory Faith provides the way through.

Love: We'll Never be Lonely Again

Do you remember the first time you consciously realized that you were deeply loved by someone? That someone may have been a parent or grandparent, a sibling, a friend, or a person who would one day become your spouse. Think about it for a moment. Who was this person and what was the event that made you realize such deep love? That memory can be a highlight for you. Through that act of love, you were graced with the opportunity to know deep human love.

I remember an event from my early teen years. A person from the neighborhood came to our house and told my father that I had broken her window. My father listened to the person's complaint, and then told her in my presence that he would check it out. After the person left, he sat down with me and asked me if I had broken the window. The facts were that I had not broken the window, was nowhere near the location of the window when it was broken, and had no idea who had broken it. As I started to cry, thinking he would never believe me, I told him I was not guilty. He believed me! Then he took me straight to the neighbor's house and told her I didn't do it. She of course did not believe him, but there was not much she could do about it. As we walked home together in silence, I felt enveloped in my father's trust and love. That event is a benchmark event because it was the first time I became aware in a concrete way of my father's deep love for me. I felt affirmed by my father through that event. In a sense, by taking the risk of believing me rather than the neighbor, he showed his love for me and his confidence in me. I really got a boost of self-esteem in that encounter. Oh, and the guy who did break the window was caught the next week breaking another window in the neighborhood. The neighbor never came over and apologized for accusing me. Oh well . . . that really doesn't matter, because the memory helped change my life. Memories are important, aren't they?

Do you remember the first time you consciously realized that you were deeply loved by God? Think about it a moment. What was the occasion? Whom or what did God use to show you His love? That memory can be a highlight for you because through it, God gave you an opportunity to respond to His deep love in such a way that you were given assurance of your place in God's Kingdom.

I recall an event where God made known His deep love for me. While I was in Vietnam, I attended the chapel in our compound. The chapel was a basic structure with a rough wooden floor and plywood walls that went up about three feet from the floor with screens going up the rest of the way to the beginning of the roof. A galvanized steel roof completed the structure, with a rustic wooden cross adorning the top. Inside were wooden benches without backrests, a rough altar and pulpit, and a small field organ. Our Air Group Chaplain led the services and his enlisted assistant led the singing. This chapel was a refuge for those of us who flew and those who worked on the aircraft of Marine Aircraft Group Twelve. Every night, we flyers were launched into the air in "airborne coffins" full of death and destruction. Our primary objective was to deliver this death and destruction on enemy truck convoys carrying weapons and supplies down the Ho Chi Minh Trail to resupply the North Vietnamese Army in its fight with South Vietnamese and American forces. Our second objective was to bomb transshipment points where the supplies and ammo were stockpiled. In order to accomplish these objectives, we had to avoid extremely effective anti-aircraft artillery, and then fly back and land our "coffins" safely on our airstrip. The stress level was high, and that is putting it mildly. So the chapel held great significance for us. Through hymns, sermons, and prayers, the worship services allowed for some cathartic moments on our part.

One night in the chapel, we sang a hymn I had never heard before. And the words spoke God's love to me in a powerful way. As I began to sing the words, *"When I survey the wondrous cross where the young Prince of Glory died,"* I was caught up in the story . . . *"My richest gain I count but loss, and pour contempt on all my pride."* It was as if I was in heaven with the angels, pouring out praise to God. *"Were the whole realm of nature mine, that were an offering far too small; Love so amazing, so divine, demands my soul, my life, my all"* (*Army & Navy Hymnal*, Isaac Watts).

As we finished the hymn, I realized I was weeping with a happiness I could not account for. For a moment, I sensed that God was right there with me!

Just before we sang that hymn, the chaplain had preached a wonderful sermon on God's love for us, and God's desire that we repent of our sins and allow Him to love us. As he preached, I admitted to God that I had let Him down; I repented and accepted His love for me. I could sense God's love filling me. And so when we sang that hymn following the sermon, the words leapt right off the page into my heart! The hymn became a love song to our Lord, a way to thank Him for the great love He showed me on the cross. After the service I copied the words on a sheet of paper. For many days thereafter, I sang the hymn when I was alone. I even sent the words to my wife and explained to her how God had ministered to me through them. I still remember the warmth I felt singing that hymn to God! It is a memory I will never forget; it strengthens my faith. That is what Memory Faith is all about.

Chapter Eight

Memory Faith
Caught Napping

Limitations of Memory Faith

As important as memories are to our faith journey, there is a downside to them. Memory Faith can also become a trap keeping us from living into Miracle Faith. We can get caught in a time warp, and spend the rest of our lives reliving that important "memory" so many years ago when God became real to us. Let's take a look at the limitations of Memory Faith, so that we can stay out of this trap!

A colleague of mine—let's call him Tom—was involved in a ministry that encouraged us to tell our faith story and the circumstances of our conversion to Jesus Christ. Tom had a conversion experience years before when he was in college. While it had been a dramatic conversion, it had not been a miraculous one. After he had been in college for a year, and was questioning the existence of God, he became involved in a campus ministry program that sponsored retreats at a conference center on the beach. Tom went on one such retreat. There was good preaching aimed at helping people commit their lives to Christ, and plenty of time to walk the beach and consider the content of the sermons. While walking alone on the beach one night after one of the sermons, Tom reached that "aha" moment when he verbally gave his life to Jesus and invited Him to come in as Lord and Savior. He later let the retreat leader know about his experience, and was given high public praise for the "miracle" of having that conversion experience with God. This, then, became the high-water mark in Tom's spiritual pilgrimage.

But over the years, and each time Tom retold his story, the conversion experience took on more and more of a miraculous tone. One day, Tom's wife asked me what she could do to help him. "Tom has blown this conversion experience way out of proportion," Mildred sighed. "I was going out with him when this happened, so I know what he reported at the time. What I hear him saying now does not even resemble what he first said happened when he went through that experience. He never mentioned audibly hearing God talk to him; he never mentioned that God told him to open his Bible and it automatically opened to Romans 10:9, 10. Why is Tom exaggerating, and what can I do to help him tell the truth?"

I wish I could tell you that there has been some resolution here, but I suspect that Tom is still telling his story, exaggerated as it may be, and actually believing it happened that way. But what I have come to realize is that, because of our deep need to feel important, we can consciously or even unconsciously change our memories so that they point more to us than to God.

Memory Faith can see us through a multitude of difficulties. But if our faith is tied only to a dramatic memory, our minds can play tricks on us. Staking your life on a memory can move you in one of two directions. The memory either becomes dim or it becomes exaggerated. This can happen to every account in our "memory bank." Have you ever had a reunion with an old friend and had the conversation drift back in time to an event the two of you shared? You remember every detail of the event, including the temperature at the time, what you were both wearing, and what significant world catastrophe was taking place at the time. But as you try to relive the event, you are staggered by your friend's lack of memory of any details! The memory seems to have faded completely from his mind. It was either not that big an event for him; or maybe because this person seldom relives past events, the event just faded into the dusty archives of his brain, never to be retrieved.

Or, how about sitting in a group, listening to a friend relate a dangerous incident the two of you shared some time ago? As she tells the story, you begin to realize that she is not telling it right at all. She is embellishing her part in the event and diminishing yours! As you try to protest, she shouts you down and accuses you of having CRS (Can't Remember Stuff). When later in private, you challenge your friend about her rendition of the incident, you are floored to discover that she really believes it happened just the way she told it, and that she is greatly offended by your attempt to change the story. One of you has a memory problem, and you know it's not you.

Yes, memories are important, but they are not always reliable. Unless we relive a memory honestly and regularly, it will become either faded or inflated!

Scripture Memories— Photos or Fish Stories?

Our forebears who put the scriptures together intuitively knew that. So they sat around the campfire each night and retold the old memories—honestly and regularly. And then their kids did the same thing, adding new memories from their lifetimes, on and on down through the generations. And when it was written down, there were people around who could say, "Hey, wait a minute! You didn't write that memory correctly!"

When some biblical scholars tell me I can't trust the miraculous accounts in the Bible because they are obviously exaggerated memories, my 21st century mind wants to agree. I think, "Sure. These are fish stories—getting bigger and bigger with each telling. But when I study the culture in which the events occurred so long ago, my trust in the Holy Spirit's process of writing scripture is restored. These people cared for their memories! In our age, we are not as good at "memory keeping." Our memories tend to be faded or inflated.

Let's look at a historical event from the Old Testament. In doing so, we can get a sense of how the Israelites kept their memories carefully, wrapping them in a beautiful box with red ribbon, taking them out regularly and honestly to look at them. Let's talk about "Elijah the Prophet and the Gigantic Rain Storm."

Little Guy—Big Storm—Big Memory!

The Background: Elijah the Prophet lived in the ninth century, B.C. in what was then called the Northern Kingdom of Israel. The setting is Israel, some four hundred years after Joshua's miraculous crossing of the Jordan River. Elijah the Prophet is portrayed as the hero, and

Ahab and Jezebel, King and Queen of the Northern Kingdom of Israel, are portrayed as the villains.

The Story: Elijah is upset that Ahab and Jezebel are leading the people of Israel away from the Lord God and encouraging them to worship the local gods, in particular Baal. Elijah prophesies regularly against them, and Ahab is getting sick of it. The particular event we are discussing here occurs after a three-year drought. Elijah had prophesied the drought as God's judgment upon Ahab. Ahab of course was not pleased with the prophesy, nor with the drought that followed the prophesy. He hated Elijah, called him "Troubler of Israel," and had his henchmen looking all over Israel to murder Elijah.

Now after three years of drought, Elijah has a sense from God that the drought will end only after the false-god Baal is publicly defeated. Elijah comes out of hiding and challenges the 450 prophets of Baal to a contest of faith. In a dramatic and stunning victory over them, Elijah shows that God's power is greater than that of the false-god Baal. Thus purged of the filth of these prophets, God can now send rain to refresh the earth.

Well, let's tune in to the story from First Kings:

And Elijah said to Ahab, "Go up, eat and drink; for there is a sound of the rushing of rain." So Ahab went up to eat and drink.

And Elijah went up to the top of Carmel; and he bowed himself down upon the earth, and put his face between his knees. And he said to his servant, "Go up now, look toward the sea."

And he went up and looked, and said, "There is nothing." And he said, "Go again seven times." And at the seventh time he said, "Behold, a little cloud like a man's hand is rising out of the sea."

And Elijah said, "Go up, say to Ahab, 'Prepare your chariot and go down, lest the rain stop you.'"

And in a little while the heavens grew black with clouds and wind, and there was a great rain. And Ahab rode and went to Jezreel. And the hand of the Lord was on Elijah; and he girded up his loins and ran before Ahab to the entrance of Jezreel.

1 Kings 18:41-46

What a story! And told with drama and great detail! Elijah has just had a dramatic victory over 450 prophets and the evil god they believed in! As he then walks to the top of Mount Carmel with his servant, he is filled with emotion. At the top, he is so overcome that he fears he will throw up. He does what you and I would do—bends down and puts his head between his knees. He is so overcome, he can't even watch for the coming storm he has predicted. He sends his servant to look west and watch for the hoped for storm brewing over the Mediterranean. While Elijah waits, he wonders if God will come through—will the storm really come? He is filled with angst. Grasping for hope, he tells the servant to look "seven times," symbolic of the perfect number—in God's perfect timing, the storm will come. Sure enough, on the seventh look, the servant sees something out over the sea, but it is so small—the size of a hand.

But it is enough for Elijah. Knowing that God is in fact acting, he sends word to King Ahab to get his chariot out of there and to head for Jezreel before he is overcome by the approaching storm. Note that at this point there is no sign of rain. Ahab has enough faith to believe that Elijah may just be right. Why else would he follow Elijah's instructions? After witnessing the victory Elijah has just had over the prophets of Baal, Ahab decides to give Elijah the benefit of the doubt. He sets out in his chariot. With darkening skies and a gully washer of a storm boring in on him, he roars across the plain toward Jezreel, only to be amazed when he sees an eighty-year-old prophet named Elijah outracing him on foot!

This event gives us a word-picture of an event in history meant to encourage and teach. Can't you hear that story being told over and over again in school and over the campfire? Some present day Bible scholars would tell us that this is simply a story without fact; that it is an embellished folk-tale, manufactured to mobilize and motivate the Israelites. But if we believe the importance the Israelites placed on memories, how they protected their memories by honestly and regularly repeating them, we can see something serious here. This memory has not been inflated nor has it faded. Those who believe that the Bible should be purged of any "myths" or "wonder stories" that might work against acceptance of the Bible by the scientific community should rethink their position. Much in life today does not seem to fit all the laws of nature. After all, from a purely sociological viewpoint, people in various cultures can, without meteorological instrumentation, predict rain these days, and the rain comes! Why not Elijah back then? We need to focus on the integrity of the Israelite memory bank, and the integrity of the Holy Spirit's action in forming the Word of God.

Then we can be more open to the fact that God is still active in the world. Sometimes God acts in accordance with the laws of nature, and sometimes He lays those laws aside and produces a giant miracle!

Our Personal Memories— Do We Care for Them?

Because we are not good at memory keeping, we allow them to be inflated or faded. I have good memories regarding my early journey with the Lord, and how He made Himself known in my life. But one day I woke up "without memory." You see, I had been preaching for a number of years, but had long since ceased sharing my personal faith story. My sermons had become intellectual and impersonal, and then they became somewhat predictable and dry. I simply stopped "remembering," and stopped being personal. I had, through ordination and parish life, transferred my faith from a tender relationship with Jesus to a rocky relationship with the parish. I had moved from personal faith to professional faith teaching. I had so taken Jesus for granted that I had consigned Him to being a plate of bread and a cup of wine. Due to my refusal to share personal faith memories, I had "forgotten" the great story of the God-Dave encounter. I was in need of renewal! The memories had faded.

On the other hand, there are those who get stuck in the backwater of faith because their whole take on faith is tied to a single conversion event. Some churches so emphasize conversion as a one-time, never to be repeated event that they unwittingly freeze people into Memory Faith. So these faith-filled people get stuck there and cannot move on to Miracle Faith. Since their dramatic conversion years ago, which they may or may not have considered miraculous, they have not progressed at all. Wind them up in a prayer group, Bible study, or faith sharing, and they will tell you about their dramatic conversion years ago. Their Memory Faith is frozen at a single date and event in history, and they have had no desire to move on to deeper faith. So they do not move into the realm of active guidance by the Holy Spirit. And they do not ask daily for the infilling of the Holy Spirit. They are in fact suspicious of the whole concept of the Spirit filling people, thinking it is a Pentecostal plot to make them speak in tongues. And so they miss the blessing, preferring instead to live in a world of "Jesus and me," and their ministry consists of just telling their story. They are stuck in Memory Faith!

Now, don't get me wrong. I consider Memory Faith important. My conversion in 1968 in Vietnam is a very important memory for me. I tell my conversion story frequently. The story I tell has helped other people to come to a personal relationship with Jesus Christ. But I simply must move forward, without forgetting the memory of my conversion, into a deeper faith in God. I have to move into a daily dose of Miracle Faith. The threat we all face is the risk of getting so stuck in the memories of our conversion— Memory Faith—that we miss the opportunity of enjoying the intimacy the Miracle Maker wishes for us.

The Road to Miracle Faith and Miracle Ministry

Chapter Nine

The Rubber is Hitting the Road!

The Gift of Miracle Faith

So we've looked at the ups and downs of Memorial Faith and Memory Faith, of their power and of their traps. Let's see how Memorial Faith and Memory Faith can be doors that usher us into that most wonderful stage of faith. It is time to look at the gift of Miracle Faith.

I have already mentioned Bill, my pilot from Vietnam. After our tour of duty in Vietnam, we both returned to the states for further duty. Several years later, I became a theological student in the Washington, D.C. area. Bill was also assigned in the D.C. area. He and his wife and four children lived within easy driving range, and so my wife and I became their family friends. Although Bill was only beginning to trust in God, his wife was a strong, church-going believer. Our conversations about faith continued—Bill was ever the tutor—critically analyzing what I said, not to be argumentative but to assist me in developing into a good pastor. I valued our discussions.

One day, Bill's wife was doing her "Mama Car Pool" thing when her car crashed and she died shortly thereafter—on her birthday. Bill suddenly found himself a thirty-eight year-old widower with four small children! Somehow we all got through the shock, the visits, and the funeral. And Bill was faced with a crumbled world.

The night before the funeral, Bill sat beside the casket and made some promises to his wife. He would raise those kids in the faith she so loved. He would be a good parent, and raise good God-loving kids. And he would do all he could to join her in heaven. He promised her with all the faith he could muster.

And his life started over—the difficult life of being a single dad. He took the kids to church—every week. He took them to religious education—every week. He helped them with their homework, went to their meetings and athletic contests, taught them what it meant to live an honest, productive life. He retired early from the Marine Corps so that he could exercise closer supervision and loving, firm care for his kids.

And he began to ponder what his wife's death was really all about and what he could learn from it. Slowly he began to realize that God was using the car accident to get his attention. God did not cause the accident, but He did use it to reach out to Bill. Bill had been so deeply in unbelief that conversion could only come after the very timbers of his life were shaken. Notice: I did not say that God purposely staged the death of Marcia so that Bill would be converted. But God did bring good out of the accident—He used the results of that accident to reach down into Bill's soul and pull out Miracle Faith. In the years that followed the accident, Bill slowly but surely drew close to God. Marcia called across the Great Divide—"Come, Bill. Love God. He loves you! Respond!"

The day finally came when Bill surrendered his life to God and accepted Christ as his Lord and Savior. He was received into the Church, and has not fallen away from God. He is a believing Christian today. His kids are Christ-believing adults. He fulfilled his promise to his wife. God touched him with Miracle Faith.

God has been doing this stuff for years! He's good at it! It started in the Bible.

The Great Damascus Road Miracle

Saul was a person of faith. But for many years he had only Memorial Faith. He did not have Miracle Faith. According to snippets of autobiography found in his Epistles and a history written by Luke in the Book of Acts, he was a first century Hellenistic Jew born in Tarsus, a city in what is today south-central Turkey, and was given the good Jewish name Saul. He was without doubt brought up in a Jewish section of Tarsus, and educated by the local rabbi. As a teenager, he was sent by his well-to-do parents to Jerusalem to get a "proper" Jewish education. Saul claimed the famous Rabbi Gamaliel as his teacher. So he received a proper education, and was very fervent in studying Judaism. By his own admission, he was therefore very much against the followers of Jesus, whom he considered heretics.

But it seems apparent from reading his letters and the accounts of his activities in the Book of Acts that his early faith was based on study and liturgy, not on experience with God. It is probable that while he did have "head knowledge" about the faith called Judaism, he had little "heart knowledge" of the God of Judaism. The faith he had developed was strong on history but weak on experience, strong on ethics but weak on relationships. His faith was based on an understanding of the historic nature of God's dealings with the People of Israel—Memorial Faith. He had not had a personal encounter with the God he studied—he did not know the miracle of God invading the universe to embrace him—no Miracle Faith. And I suspect he was not really happy or personally sustained by daily times of personal prayer and intimacy with God.

Saul was very protective of the orthodoxy of Judaism. So he joined a number of Jewish leaders in Jerusalem who sought to wipe out this new Christ-oriented Jewish sect. His intention was to protect the historic faith of Judaism. It was on one of his forays to wipe out the Jewish sect of Jesus-followers that his Memorial Faith was turned to Miracle faith. Let's check in now. Let's travel back in time to a lonely, dusty road that ran from Jerusalem to Damascus.

> *All this time Saul was breathing down the necks of the Master's disciples, out for the kill. He went to the Chief Priests and got arrest warrants to take to the meeting places in Damascus so that if he found anyone there belonging to the Way, whether men or women, he could arrest them and bring them to Jerusalem.*

He set off. When he got to the outskirts of Damascus, he was suddenly dazed by a blinding flash of light. As he fell to the ground, he heard a voice: "Saul, Saul, why are you out to get me?"

He said, "Who are you, master?"

"I am Jesus, the One you're hunting down.

I want you to get up and enter the city. In the city you'll be told what to do next."

> *His companions stood there dumb-struck—they could hear the sound, but couldn't see anyone—while Saul, picking himself up off the ground, found himself stone blind. They had to take him by the hand and lead him into Damascus. He continued blind for three days. He ate nothing, drank nothing.*
>
> Acts 9:1-9—*The Message*

Now this is Miracle Faith at work! When people tell me that they have heard an audible voice from God, I often wonder if they are suffering some form of hallucinatory behavior. And probably some are. But are they all? Saul had great credibility among his fellow Christians, and is considered one of the greatest missionaries of all time. He said that he heard the audible voice of Jesus! Was he speaking symbolically or literally? The way Saul speaks of his experience, it does not appear that he wanted us to take it symbolically. Saul believed that he heard a voice, and that it was the voice of Jesus! This can only mean that we are in the world of "miracle" here. Saul experienced one of the greatest miracles of all time! But think for a moment about what Saul suffered in experiencing the miracle. Would you like to go through that Damascus Road experience in order to get in contact with the Living God? Be struck blind, not knowing if you will ever see again? Seems frightening, doesn't it?

But that is what it took for God to get Saul's attention, and so that is what God did. On a dusty, country road, God took time out from managing the universe in order to do business with one of His children. But what happened next? Let's return to the text.

> So Ananias went and found the house, placed his hands on blind Saul, and said, "Brother Saul, the Master sent me, the same Jesus you saw on your way here. He sent me so you could see again and be filled with the Holy Spirit." No sooner were the words out of his mouth then something like scales fell from Saul's eyes—he could see again! He got to his feet, was baptized, and sat down with them to a hearty meal.
>
> Saul spent a few days getting acquainted with the Damascus disciples, but then went right to work, wasting no time, preaching in the meeting places that this Jesus was the Son of God.
>
> Acts 9:17-20—*The Message*

Miracle of Miracles! This frightening antagonist of Christ has now been set free from the slavery to a cold, hard Memorial Faith, so that he can personally experience the One, True God. After spending three days in a blind state, neither eating nor drinking, Saul is visited by a humble Christian gentleman named Ananias. Ananias is God's instrument for healing and converting Saul. Ananias simply lays his hands on Saul as a symbol of God's healing power, asks that Saul allow himself to be filled with the Strengthening Spirit of God, and then watches in amazement as scales fall from Saul's eyes and Saul can now see clearly both physically *and* spiritually. By the way, some Bible commentators have suspected that St. Paul's "thorn in the flesh" was an eye problem. Could this have been a lifetime condition, which served to continually remind St. Paul of that Damascus Road experience?

Back to the story—Saul can see again! And what does he do next? He believes Jesus! He immediately allows himself to be liturgically baptized into the faith of Jesus, and he begins witnessing to his fellow Jews that Jesus is the Son of God.

Saul's new Miracle Faith led him to a whole new life. Later, God changed his name, from the

Jewish "Saul" to the Gentile "Paul," thus expressing the miracle of the conversion of a self-righteous Jew into a Gentile-loving Christian Missionary. This is Miracle Faith in action.

This is the faith God intends for each one of us. But like Paul, we often need a powerful turn-around experience and healing in order to claim that Miracle Faith.

God Wants Miracle Faith for You

There are six billion stories like St. Paul's on planet Earth. Mine is but one of them, but it is an important one. It is important because my story is "God's Story." It is God's history—the history of how the God of the Universe has stooped down, looked at this little creature on planet Earth and said, "David, I love you. Let me show you how much I love you—look at my Son on the cross."

When the God who hurled galaxies into existence can get that personally involved with His human beings, it is indeed a miracle! The Holy Scriptures teach me that God the Father wants to have a personal and continuing encounter with each one of His children, has provided the means for this encounter through the cross of Jesus, and empowers us through His Holy

Spirit to respond with penitent and accepting hearts.

When Paul spoke of his "defining moment" with Jesus, he was not just play-acting or trying to build a sensational story to boost book sales. He was sharing with us a profound personal experience in the hope that we would be encouraged to allow God to become profoundly personal with us as well. The Lord Jesus Christ wants us to have Miracle Faith. Why else would He have said the things He said, done the things He did, died the death He died, and rose the way He rose? The God Incarnate, the Great Miracle, loves you and me so much that nothing will stop Him from giving us the opportunity to be set free from our self-imposed prison of selfishness and sin. Just as God healed St. Paul by causing the scales to fall from his eyes, so God heals us by causing the spiritual scales, or blinders, to fall from our eyes.

Healing—A Context for Miracle Faith

"God heals us?" Hmm. Lest the word "healing" cause confusion in our minds, let's look at it in the context of the subject at hand. Healing is the vehicle by which Miracle Faith becomes an integral part of our lives. Before Miracle Faith can take place, miracle healing must happen. I am not talking so much about the event we sometimes see on television: the white-suited evangelist standing in the stadium, loudly commanding God to "heal" the crippled person in front of him. I'm not making a judgment on that kind of healing; I'm just not focusing on it here. When I use the word "healing" in the context of this chapter, I am talking about the deep inner healing that thaws our cold, restless hearts and melts them into joy and peace.

As a liturgical Christian, I often see God's miraculous healing at work sacramentally. In looking at the two Gospel Sacraments (called Ordinances by some Protestants)—Holy Baptism and Holy Eucharist—and the five Sacramental Rites—Confirmation, Penance, Holy Unction, Holy Orders, and Holy Matrimony—I see wonderful opportunities for God to perform healing miracles in the lives of His people. God has been known to heal us through the Sacraments. Here follow some examples.

A person coming forward to be Baptized or Confirmed is often healed of a memory of abandonment, as they hear the priest or bishop say, "You are sealed by the Holy Spirit in Baptism and marked as Christ's own forever." A woman who had been adopted as an infant once told me that she had never been able to reconcile her situation as an adopted child until the day she was confirmed as a young adult. As the bishop laid his hands on her head and prayed, "Defend, O Lord, your servant with your heavenly grace, that she may continue yours for ever, and daily increase in your Holy Spirit more and more, until she comes to your everlasting kingdom," she literally felt the Father's arms close around her. Her fear of abandonment subsided, and in the days that followed, she lost the fear she had carried since childhood. The Christian community, emphasizing authentic relationships in Christ, brought her to a new level of feeling accepted. She considered it a miracle. She was healed. In Baptism and Confirmation, we are assured of God's loving and comforting parenthood, lived out in the Christian community of the Church, showing us a love that will never abandon us.

A person receiving the Sacrament of Holy Communion can be healed from a memory of bitterness and sorrow. In receiving the Body and Blood, we realize that Jesus is pouring Himself into us—into our lives and souls—melting the pain and sorrow of our past. A husband and wife attended a Marriage Encounter Weekend my wife and I led. The Weekend concluded with Holy

Communion. The husband had not received Communion in many years, but on this weekend, after rediscovering the love he had for his wife, and rediscovering the love God had for him, he decided to receive the Sacrament. Tears ran down his cheeks as he invited Jesus to come again into his life and be Lord. Receiving the Body and Blood of Jesus in the bread and wine was a tangible way for him to experience the healing presence of Christ in his life and in his marriage. It can bring the same miracle to your life and mine.

A person receiving Absolution (or assurance of God's forgiveness) after making a Confession is often healed from a memory of guilt related to sinful actions, thoughts, or words. A woman, who had years ago fallen into a short adulterous affair, had suffered from her sense of guilt ever since, and ended up resenting herself for her lack of faithfulness to her husband. Finally, in the context of a parish retreat, she was able to confess her sin to God in the presence of a priest. She has given me permission to tell you that as she heard the assurance of God's forgiveness, her life changed immediately. A great weight was lifted from her. She was able to better understand why she had fallen into the relationship, and as she finally believed that God had forgiven her and put that sin away from her forever, she was then able to forgive herself. Her new life was marked by joy, assurance, and a new love for her husband. She was healed. God wants that miracle for each one of us.

A person experiencing the Grace of God given in the wedding ceremony—Holy Matrimony— is often healed from a memory of aimlessness or walking through the "wilderness of life" alone. Once, after I had conducted the Marriage Eucharist for a young couple, the husband described the healing he had received as he heard his intended say to him, "In the Name of God, I, Jane, take you, John, to be my husband, to have and to hold from this day forward, for better for worse, for richer for poorer, in sickness and in health, to love and to cherish, until we are parted by death. This is my solemn vow." He said that as he looked into her eyes and heard her heart-felt pledge to him, it was like he was looking into the eyes of Jesus—and all the horrors of loneliness and aimless wandering melted away as he felt himself totally wrapped in God's love in the face of his wife. What a miracle for you and me!

A person receiving the gift of Holy Orders (or ordination) is often healed from a memory of being overly self-indulgent, as the realization comes that having received the gift of ordination, life will now involve giving first and receiving second. When I was ordained to the Priesthood, I felt a great weight upon my head as my bishop and fellow priests laid their hands on me and the bishop spoke the words making me a priest. For me, that great weight symbolized Jesus laying his cross on me as he walked the Via Dolorosa to Calvary. I knew he was depending on me to assist him, just as he had depended on Simon of Cyrene that first Good Friday so long ago. At the moment of ordination I knew that the Priesthood was not to be some glorified holy life centering on me and my inspiring sermons—it was not to be primarily a receiving kind of thing. It was to be a giving kind of thing, a giving of myself to Christ and His Body the Church. That moment was a giant step in being healed of self-indulgence. In place of the "illness of self-indulgence," I received a desire to serve, a desire to dedicate my life to the service of God's people. God wants to heal all of us of our self-centeredness so He can truly fit us for His service, whether ordained or lay ministers.

And finally, God has healed many people through the Sacrament of Unction, the anointing with Holy Oil and laying-on-of-hands for healing of physical, emotional, spiritual, demonic, or relational ills. Many people have received healing of memories in the areas of worthlessness and hopelessness. A man came forward at one of our healing services and complained of an extremely bad back. He had not been able to sleep for many days, and would sometimes pass out from the pain. As the bishop and the healing team anointed him with Holy Oil and prayed for healing, his back pain went away. That night he slept like a baby, and has continued to do so in the several years since he was healed. But perhaps the real miracle was the healing he received in the context of his own attitude of hopelessness. He had consigned himself to a lifetime of pain. He felt hopeless and worthless. God healed him of that. He developed Miracle Faith, and has been growing in that faith ever since. God wants to heal us of our sense of worthlessness so that we can shout from the rooftops that God is a God of hope!

Are you in need of healing in soul, body, mind, relationship, or spirit? Why not make yourself available for God's healing? Seek out opportunities to lay your pain at the feet of Jesus. That opportunity may come as you allow someone to pray for you privately or at a healing service. It may come when you receive the right medical treatment for your ailment. It may come as a result of good counseling. It may come while reading the Bible or listening to a sermon or to a Christian radio/TV show. It may come in a quiet moment shared between you and the Lord. Whatever the opportunity, work on developing an understanding that God is always the healer, and that He is healing you in order to give you Miracle Faith! When you have Miracle Faith, you can then develop Miracle Ministry.

Jim and a Healing Miracle

Jim was a quiet boy in school, as well as at home. His father had died when he was three, and he was raised by his domineering mother. He had practically no friends, and he soon retreated into a fantasy world where he pretended he lived in a "normal" family with a loving mother and father. As he grew into his mid-teens, he discovered that high school was a jungle for him. The athletes picked on him without mercy, calling him "fag" and other degrading names. Girls never even looked at him. Jim became a loner. He wandered the halls and classrooms each day, trying to avoid trouble-makers, and waiting for graduation when he would not have to be there anymore. His mother was not a churchgoer, so she passed on no faith teachings to him. He was never once taken to a church, not even for a wedding or a funeral. In his sophomore year of high school, his forty-year-old uncle took an interest in him, telling Jim's mother he would give him some fathering. Unfortunately for Jim, the "fathering" turned out to be a homosexual relationship. After several years of this, Jim grew more and more uncomfortable and tried to end the relationship. But Jim's uncle convinced him that his sexual orientation was homosexual, and that Jim should get used to the lifestyle. The uncle began taking Jim to gay bars and got him involved in a number of gay relationships.

Jim went to college mostly to get away from his uncle. But after several months of finding himself once again the butt of jokes in the dorm, and finding no friends, he fell back into the gay lifestyle as a way to cope with life. He had numerous partners over his four years in college, but fortunately never contracted HIV / AIDS. In his quiet moments, he would disappear into his fantasy world, where his imaginary father and mother would read to him, take him to ball games, and just love him. Jim suspected he was slightly delusional, but was afraid to get help. So he limped along through life.

College graduation was the door to a career in graphic design, and Jim was hired by a firm on the other side of the nation. Once again, he resolved that he would end his gay lifestyle. But alas, his new job did not include any opportunities for him to develop lasting friendships. And the gay bar was just a couple blocks from his office.

One day, Jim got into a conversation with a co-worker who had the reputation of being a religious fanatic. George was a deacon at an area church. The conversation was positive and friendly. Other conversations followed. Neither propositioned the other. They just talked. After a month of developing a friendship, George invited Jim home for dinner, where George's wife and children treated him with friendly respect. For the first time in his life, Jim caught a glimpse of what he had always considered a "normal" family. "They all seem to treat each other so nicely," thought Jim. "Can this be real?"

Jim and George became friends in the weeks that followed, and Jim enjoyed many evenings at dinner with George and Barbara. Jim was beginning to love this family. He found he was not retreating to his fantasy world nearly as often as he used to, and he was losing his desire to hit the gay bars.

Then one day, George told Jim that his church was having a special potluck supper and worship service on Wednesday night—would he like to be George's guest? Jim didn't know what to say. He didn't know much about churches, except that he thought they were rather condemning in their view toward gays. But his trust in George made him say that he would accompany George to church.

That visit to the church changed Jim's life. The church members treated him well. They seemed genuinely glad to have him there. The worship service was spirited and joyful. The Bible teaching was nothing like he thought it might be. Instead of feeling condemned for his sinfulness, he felt enveloped in God's love!

Thus began a period of discipleship for Jim. He joined a men's Bible class at the church, and soon made a commitment to Jesus Christ. But he did so without settling his sexual questions. Although he was no longer involved in gay sex, he was not sure what to do with his background, and he was not sure how he would handle himself in the future if his relationship with the church did not last.

He broke down in George's home one night and poured out his pent-up guilt for indulging in so many illicit relationships. He cried and cried in George's arms, as a child does in the arms of a parent. In a sense, George "re-parented" Jim that night. Instead of using physical affection as a way into a gay relationship, George gave gentle counsel and assurance. He let Jim know that his repentance would bring complete forgiveness by God. George led Jim in the sinner's prayer whereby Jim confessed every known sin he could remember, thanked Jesus for dying on the cross for him, and asked Jesus to come in and clean him up. All the wounds that had been inflicted on Jim and that Jim had in turn inflicted on others were healed. In the months that followed, Jim received good counseling and settled the sexual conflicts within.

Today, twenty years later, Jim is a pastor! He is kind and gentle, and well-loved by his congregation. He is preaching the Gospel. He has not returned to the gay scene. I don't know all there is to know about sexual orientation and behavior, or whether homosexual people are capable of or even desirous of changing their lifestyle. But I know Jim changed. I worked with him for several years, and am most impressed with his heroic stand for the Gospel.

That's Miracle Faith! Which issues into Miracle Ministry! You're going to love the next chapter!

Chapter Ten

Miracle Ministry— God's Gift to Us

*Almighty and eternal God, so draw our hearts
to you, so guide our minds, so fill our imagi-
nations, so control our wills, that we may be
wholly yours, utterly dedicated to you; and
then use us, we pray, as you will, and always
to your glory and the welfare of your people;
through our Lord and Savior Jesus Christ.
Amen.* BCP, 833

Ministry Without Miracle Faith

Jack started his ordained ministry in true
"rugged individual" fashion. He refused to pray
before meetings or other Christian activities.
His pet statement was, "God has given us all the
talent we need to do this. Let's not hide behind
prayers, and then blame God when we don't
have the 'oomph' to carry it through to success."
Jack never had more than a deistic view of God
in the first place. That was what he grew up
believing, and three years in seminary gave him
no reason to change his mind about it. As a
deist, he believed that God had scientifically
created the world, and had then put enough
intelligence within humankind to allow them to
bring the Creation to fruition. So, according to
Jack, God was no longer involved in the Creation.
Whatever happened on earth was up to the

human beings God had made. And Jack's job was to get these humans moving! Period. End of conversation!

In Jack's first ten years out of seminary, he ran his parish like a business. He saw himself as the CEO of the organization, and he organized the Vestry like a Board of Directors. His goal was to increase the membership and the budget of the parish. By using sound management principles, he began to see results in both increased membership and increased budget. He trained the Vestry to use carefully formulated goals and objectives in maintaining their ministries, with semi-annual evaluations as to how they were doing. For all intents and purposes, the parish was becoming a successful business.

But Jack did not teach anyone to pray, and he was not interested in starting Bible studies. He was interested in Christian Education programs only if they showed Jesus as a great teacher of human effectiveness; he was not interested in showcasing Jesus as a compassionate Savior.

While Jack was comfortable at cocktail parties, social outings, and business meetings, he was becoming uncomfortable with certain other aspects of parish life—leading worship, praying with the hospitalized, and giving spiritual direction. He bristled if anyone mentioned a need for spiritual renewal in the parish.

In order to deal with mounting criticism regarding his reluctance to utilize pastoral skills, he raised enough money to hire an Assistant Rector, and quickly gave her those responsibilities. Although he continued to show up at the worship services each Sunday, he changed his role to that of preacher, where he spent considerable effort motivating his parishioners to be more active in building up the parish. He allowed his Assistant to celebrate the Eucharist most of the time, and found himself lobbying for use of services that were "sermon intensive" rather than "Eucharist intensive."

Eventually Jack began to feel frustrated as more and more of his parishioners reflected what he considered a "right-wing" approach to Christianity. He noticed that his Assistant, though not given much opportunity to preach, was nonetheless winning people over to this "unsophisticated" brand of religion. Thinking he could put her in her place, he suggested that she survey the parishioners to find out what they really thought about the life of the parish. He made up the survey himself, carefully crafting the questions so that his frame of reference was the appealing one. When the results of the survey came in, Jack was aghast! In spite of the fact that he made the "right-wing" activities appear less appealing than the "solid, social" activities, the survey showed that an inordinate number of parishioners wanted Bible studies, prayer groups, and more sermons on faith issues! He felt that his Assistant had poisoned his parishioners, and found himself openly ridiculing her. He looked for ways to portray her as incompetent. This approach began to backfire on him, as parishioners moved into the role of "Protector of the Assistant."

One day, he became so upset with her that he fired her. This set about a whirlwind of resentment among the church members, with some of his disciples siding with him and a larger number of people insisting that he hire her back. All of his training in management could not sway people to his side. While he held the line and did not hire the Assistant back, he realized that he was losing his parish. He took a four-month sabbatical to analyze his position. During the sabbatical, he decided to leave parish work entirely and find something that stimulated him. Jack eventually got hired as executive director of a benevolent organization, where he could utilize his organizational skills and avoid confronting the faith issue. By this time in his life, faith in a personal God faded from his radar screen, and use of the word "ministry" to describe his work was avoided at all cost.

Jack never had Miracle Faith, and therefore he did not see Miracle Ministry. There are a lot of "Jacks" out in the parish world functioning as ordained and lay leaders. Having no reference point regarding a Miracle Faith in Christ, they reduce parish ministry to a secular business of gaining customers and increasing revenue. Miracle Ministry never enters into the life of the parish. No one gets converted, no one gets healed, no one grows in faith. God could go on an extended holiday and these folks would never know the difference. They just never really address God personally, and they neither depend upon God nor expect anything of Him. Consequently, miraculous transformation does not take place in the parish. My reading of the Bible tells me that these parishes are, at best, stagnant Christian way stations, and at worst not part of the Body of Christ!

Miracle Faith—
A Prelude to Miracle Ministry

Miracle Faith produces Miracle Ministry! I believe that God is interested in both for us.

Let's look at each of these and see how they relate directly to us.

But How Do We Catch Miracle Faith?

Miracle Faith. I am convinced that God wants us all to have Miracle Faith. Why? Because Miracle faith can produce Miracle Ministry! We may have Memorial Faith or we may have Memory Faith, or maybe even both. But what I have discovered after all these years of ministry is that Miracle Faith is God's *best* gift to us. Miracle Faith is based on a personal relationship with Jesus Christ and an active life in a parish church. Simply put: we are called by God to believe that Jesus Christ is God-in-the-flesh, who died for our sins and rose from the dead to defeat death for us. We are called by God to specifically and verbally repent of our sins and rebelliousness. And finally, we are called by God to invite Jesus Christ to come into our life as Lord and Savior, so that we can take our place as ordained and lay ministers in the Church, the Body of Christ. All of us, by virtue of our Baptism and faith commitment are called to be ministers. Our ministry may be that of a taxi driver or a housewife or the pastor of a church or a military flyer or a parent. We are all called to exercise ministry. I am not now speaking only to ordained or recognized lay leaders in the church. I am speaking to every one of us with faith!

I also want to be clear that I am not condemning the traditional rituals of the Church. I believe God has consecrated the Church, that wonderful and mystical institution, as the Body of Christ, and I believe that God gives the Church the Sacraments in order to build up the Body. The Church is God's instrument for bringing the salvation of Christ to the world. I believe it is a beautiful gift when people say they can never remember a time when they were not part of the Church Catholic.

But with all that, I am convinced from reading the scriptures and the great teachings of the ancient Catholic Fathers that the Christian faith can only come alive when people are in an ongoing relationship with the Head of the Body, Jesus Christ. And this relationship takes place outside the walls of the institution as well as within!

Speaking of beautiful traditions, read carefully the questions asked of candidates for Baptism in the Episcopal Church. When I lay this out for you, I am not saying that the Episcopal Church's way of ritualizing a person's promises to God is the only way. I am, however, showing a good example of the biblical way to appropriate the Christian Faith. The following passage from The Book of Common Prayer is a biblical summary of how people verbally accept the Christian Faith. Virtually all Christian denominations and churches ask believers to verbally accept the Christian way. Here is how the Episcopal Church does it:

Question: Do you turn to Jesus Christ and accept him as your savior?

Answer: I do.

Question: Do you put your whole trust in his grace and love?

Answer: I do.

Question: Do you promise to follow and obey him as your Lord?

Answer: I do.

BCP, 302-303

God has miraculously delivered us from the bondage of sin, and wishes to replace that bondage with freedom in Christ! We are called to acknowledge that miraculous deliverance by believing what God has done for us, and by stating verbally the above words from the Prayer Book.

Romans 10:9-10 puts it succinctly:

Because, if you confess with your lips that Jesus is Lord and believe in your heart that God raised him from the dead, you will be saved. For one believes with his heart and so is justified, and he confesses with his lips and so is saved.

An Opportunity to Sign Up for the Miracle

If you have never attempted a total surrender of your life to God in Christ, maybe you are wondering where to begin. Whether or not you have been baptized or confirmed, you may wish to reaffirm your acceptance of God's wonderful gift to you—Jesus Christ. So let's talk about that. Inviting Jesus the Christ to enter your life in a new and exciting way can be a very natural thing. After all, He loves you more than any human being has ever or ever will love you.

Why not try this? Sit down at your kitchen table or wherever you feel comfortable. Picture in your mind Jesus as you see him. Grow comfortable with Him being there with you in the chair right next to you. Look into his eyes and say a prayer something like this:

"Jesus, I welcome you into my life. I know I have sinned and been selfish, and I confess all my sins and shortcomings to you. I've been told that you died on the cross to redeem me and bring me into your Kingdom. I now turn away from all that keeps me from you, and I invite you to be my Lord and Savior—my Friend. Thank you, Lord. Amen."

Following this commitment of your life to the God of Love, you may find that your life takes on a whole new meaning. This is the beginning of Miracle Faith. You need to let your pastor or a trusted friend know that you have made a commitment to Jesus, and that you would like to meet and pray with them once a week in order to grow into this new relationship. And you can start reading the Gospel of John every day with new excitement, for there you will meet Jesus daily!

Soon you'll find that things that used to beat you down lose their power over you. Doubts that used to dog you recede in importance. Relationships that used to drive you crazy take on a new peace as you look at the Big Picture of Eternity as over against winning an argument. Miracle

Faith is believing that God is in your life twenty-four hours a day, making a difference even on days when you don't feel excited about Him!

Moving to Miracle Ministry

Miracle Ministry. Now that you've done business with God, placing Him on the throne as King of your life, and taking your ego off the throne, you can begin experiencing Miracle Ministry! Your ministry, whether it is lay or ordained, super-big or super-small, can be a Miracle.

Sure—you can decide to do it without a personal relationship with Jesus Christ. You can do it without verbally asking God to baptize you with spiritual power. You can do your ministry on your own. And while it may not produce miracles, you may find that your ministry is effective. After all, you do have talents that equip you for ministry. And if you wish, you can spend a lifetime of ordained or lay ministry based on your own strength and talents. If you have good talent and strong interpersonal skills, you will go far. But if you decide to do it that way and rely only on your persona, your success will be limited. Without giving God permission to work in, through, and with you, the chances are you will not go far with God! You may go far with people, but not with God.

I tried doing it on my own strength and skills for several years. I happen to have a lot of personal strength and probably some good interpersonal skills. I was well-liked, and I avoided offending people. So I had a good bit of success in ministry. I did in fact serve the Lord. But my motives were skewed—my reputation and good name were uppermost in my mind when I engaged in ministry. I did not want any failure because I thought it would reflect badly on me. Instead of seeking to give pleasure to God, I was seeking success for myself. As I continued on in this manner, I found that I had no time for private prayer or personal Bible study. And I definitely had no time for retreats and quiet days! The result of doing ministry in this manner was that I had little peace in my heart. I would often be bombarded by feelings of inadequacy, which would lead me to work even harder to avoid failure. When failure did come, I would shift the blame onto others or to circumstances. It got pretty awful at times and lonely as well. And so I would try again even harder. Looking back on that period of my life, I realize that doing it on my own strength led only to frustration.

I see clergy and lay people doing ministry in this manner every day; trying to do it on their own, giving only lip service to the God who is their king. Most people who continue doing ministry in this manner either burnout, or get pigeon holed in a parish they don't want anymore or a lay ministry in which they feel trapped. Some have success and continue to move up the ecclesiastical ladder. But while they may be loved by their parishioners or fellow church members, they lose the peace that passes understanding and instead, spend a lot of time protecting their space and their position. Eventually some get caught up in some sin and vanish—poof! Others drift away to non-church activities. And some minister on doggedly with that good old rugged individualism. That's sad in the long haul.

You and I have a higher calling. We are called to Miracle Ministry! Miracle Ministry is centered in the strength of God the Holy Spirit; a strength that He wants to abundantly pour into our lives. This ministry sees wonderful things happening in ministry that can only be explained by the word "miracle." Read these great words from Paul:

> *Remember, our message is not about ourselves; we're proclaiming Jesus Christ,*

the Master. All we are is messengers, errand runners from Jesus for you. It started when God said, "Light up the darkness," and our lives filled up with light as we saw and understood God in the face of Christ, all bright and beautiful.

2 Corinthians 4:6-7—*The Message*

Doing it on our strength, even with a well-written "Vision Statement," will often lead only to frustration. That is what this scripture passage is warning us about. It is when we ask God to baptize us with His life-giving Spirit that we begin to see miraculous things happen around our ministries. I have seen people changed into Christ's likeness, friends miraculously healed, social causes fruitfully proclaimed, parish budgets abundantly met, and parishes dynamically renewed!

So how do we sign up for this kind of Miracle Ministry?

An Opportunity to Sign Up for Miracle Ministry

Just as you sat with Jesus and asked Him into your life, so you can ask for the power of God the Holy Spirit to enter your life. Once again, sit quietly in your chair. Recognize that Jesus Christ, the Son of God, is present with you. Then say a prayer something like this:

> *"Jesus, I have read what you did when you walked the earth, the miracles you performed as you cared for people. You said that your followers could do the same works through the power of your Holy Spirit. I invite you right now to fill me with your Holy Spirit. I accept whatever Spiritual Gifts you want to use in my life. Just use me to make a difference in your world. Use me in Miracle Ministry. Right now, I welcome your Holy Spirit as I am filled with your power. Please show me some evidence this night or this week that you have filled me. Thank you, Jesus. Amen."*

And now trust in faith that you are filled with the Holy Spirit. You may have curious, peaceful feelings inside you right now. You may be experiencing streams of laughter or streams of tears. You may be praying in a language you do not know. Or you may be feeling nothing unusual at all. You have asked in a serious way that the Holy Spirit fill you with power. And the Holy Spirit will come through! This week, watch for God working in your life. You may be surprised at what happens. I was!

From the point when I asked God to fill me with His Holy Spirit, I tried to do *nothing* in ministry without first laying it specifically before the Lord in prayer and asking the Holy Spirit to move in that ministry. I have had to continually ask God to help me get my ego out of the way, and give God full credit. This has been difficult, so I find people of mature faith to whom I can be accountable; people I can talk to and pray with frequently.

Following these simple steps and disciplines can open your eyes to see wonderful things happen in your life. Seeming miracles can happen as you minister to your spouse, loved ones, and co-workers. You can experience Miracle Ministry not only as a pastor, but also as a truck driver! God wants to use every one of us in bringing loving bundles of miracles to the world.

I mentioned earlier in this book my college roommate, Brownie. After his helicopter crashed in Vietnam, badly burning much of his body, he spent the rest of the night evading the enemy. He was finally picked up by another rescue helicopter the next day. His burns were so bad that he was evacuated to a Navy hospital in California where he spent over a year getting massive skin grafts and trying to cope with life with a body much different than the one he had had before his crash. Brownie's faith was obviously shaken by that terrible experience. But like Bill whose life started over after the death of his wife, Brownie began to be spiritually reinvented. Over the years, God drew him closer to His bosom—God hugged him into a relationship that was unshakable. Brownie learned to fly an airplane again with hands that don't look like yours and mine, and don't operate as smoothly as ours do. He spent a good career as a corporate pilot, and touched many lives by his witness and his life. Today he is involved in a lay ministry of helping other men find dynamic faith. In the tough encounters of life, Brownie is involved with Miracle Ministry! Will you join Bill, Brownie, me, and countless others in living Miracle Faith? This wonderful Miracle Ministry?

Chapter Eleven

"Go Into the World and Make Disciples…"

Almighty God, whose Son our Savior Jesus Christ is the light of the world: Grant that your people, illumined by your Word and Sacraments, may shine with the radiance of Christ's glory, that he may be known, worshiped, and obeyed to the ends of the earth; through Jesus Christ our Lord, who with you and the Holy Spirit lives and reigns, one God, now and for ever. Amen.

BCP, 215

As I write this, I have just returned from a short-term mission trip to the Dominican Republic, where I was part of a medical mission team going into the barrios to provide medical care for those who are too poor or too remote to get any other care. Each day we would convert the nave of a church into a medical clinic. Our doctors and nurses would care for the people as they came through the door—hundreds of them. The people would receive quality scientific and faith-based medical care. As they waited, our "song man" would lead them in wonderful Gospel songs in Spanish. Some people were given hearing aids, and were able to hear the music well for the first time. And after they received their care and had their prescriptions filled, another clergy person and I would pray for each patient. This in itself was miracle enough! But the real miracle occurred among the team members. We were all so filled with Christ's love that it radiated! One evening, after we had finished the clinic, the nineteen of us on the medical mission team had an extended healing service "just for us." The other priest and I anointed each team member as they came forward and asked for particular prayers of healing. And we saw healing of souls, restoration of faith, and hope for broken relationships. After the service, several team members spoke to me about their experience and told how they sensed God's presence and healing! That's really one of the reasons I have written this book, and walked with you through these pages. Sharing these experiences with you is one of the important ways I sense God's love in action.

That experience of healing renewal in the Dominican Republic is God's plan for *each* of us—Miracle Faith played out in every day life! I have come to believe that as we live through each day with our Lord, watching for His miracles, and boldly asking Him to do miracles through us, our faith can be renewed. We can be filled with Miracle faith!

This book has been an experiment in Faith— assisting you in identifying where you are on your faith journey—Memorial Faith, Memory Faith, or Miracle Faith. I have a vision that through this book, God will reveal Himself to you in such a dynamic way that a miracle will take place in your life. The miracle? That you will integrate the best that your Memorial Faith and Memory Faith stages have offered you, that Jesus Christ will cast out whatever in those stages has crippled you or denied your progress, and that Miracle Faith will enter your consciousness in a bold and joyous way. That is my vision and prayer for you . . . and for me.

So there you have it. Memorial Faith, Memory Faith, and Miracle Faith: God's gifts to you. May you have many long years of fruitful ministry on Earth and an eternity of bliss after you leave.